P9-CDF-657

ACTION FIGURES and TOYS

SECOND WORLD WAR
and
12-inch
ACTION FIGURES

Raymond GIULIANI
Claude MESSMER
Jean-Marie MONGIN
Translated from the French by Alan McKay

The figurines on pages 40 to 50, 51, 52, 54, 62 and 63 were created by Raymond Giuliani, those on pages 51, 52, 53 and 54 to 62 by Claude Messmer and those on pages 22 to 39, 48-49 and 64 to 83 by Jean-Marie Mongin.
Except where otherwise stated photographs are by Raymond Giuliani, Jean-Louis Viau and Jean-Marie Mongin.

HISTOIRE & COLLECTIONS

A NEW DIMENSION

In this little book we are not going to present an apology for the 'military Barbie doll' — as spiteful tongues often call large-scale figurines, but rather let you see what is likely to become a real collecting phenomenon: 12-inch figurines.

A CERTAIN REVIVAL

The figurines which you are going to see all originate with the GI Joe figurines or their clones like Action Man, Action Joe and Big Jim, with which millions of young children around the world were brought up during the sixties. But as you will see throughout these pages, there is little resemblance between the American ancestor and his distant descendants coming mainly as they do from China. The choice of subjects has changed too: the American Army, its myths and heroes are no longer the only sources of inspiration. Realism or the search for realism has changed too with clothing and equipment, armament, faces. The toy side of things, this naïve side which continues to satisfy a certain number of Americans, is no longer enough for the new collectors who have been brought up on new high quality plastic figurines and irreproachable documentary support from French and English publications.

© Hasbro/GI Joe

This new generation of amateurs is looking for historical exactitude, realism and an excellent base from which it is possible to obtain a maximum of pleasure, if they want.

This new generation is made up of figurine-makers or model-makers who want to move on to other things than the 54 mm or 1/35 figurines, of those with a yearning for childhood and finally the collectors of militaria who not having a personal fortune or a large 200 m² attic in which to place their models, fall back on the large scale figurines. The latter justify their choice by saying 'since everything, or almost, in the collection of militaria is false, we may as well collect the small scale reproductions, it costs less'.

And since all the *Dragon* and *BBI* figurines have been inspired by *Histoire et Collections*, *Osprey-Men at Arms* or *Concord*, there is nothing left to prevent the collectors and amateurs of history from taking the decisive step.

SATISFYING ONE'S WISHES

It is no longer playing or even model-making which justifies the purchase of these figurines, but the desire to create a most realistic figurine, the closest thing to historical exactitude.

Here our behaviour depends on these wishes. We have only to adapt our first realisations to the skills of a budding figurine-maker. Here, our objective is to show the creations which should not take you more than three or four hours of your time. An ideal solution for enlightened amateurs.

The figurines presented in these pages however are the fruit of many hours of documentary research and gathering of spare parts.

The success of a beautiful figurine comes more from accumulating unused parts recovered from model boxes or bought loose from specialised shops than from actual manual skill. Be careful, often buying the basic figurine costs less than the total price of four or five single pieces. Tell yourself that you will be able to use all the parts one day or another. By doing this you are setting off into a leisure activity which admittedly costs a bit. But a large number of collectors will attract an importer — which is something that a lot of countries lack — with lower prices at the retailer's who, ordering greater quantities, will in turn obtain better prices which he will pass on to his customers… and so on. With a growing collection, this new phenomenon makes the amateur — you — intelligent, curious and resourceful. You have to study the period photographs carefully, do a bit of research on the uniforms, classify all the problems, make your choice and then hit hard. The range of products is big enough to satisfy all your ideas.

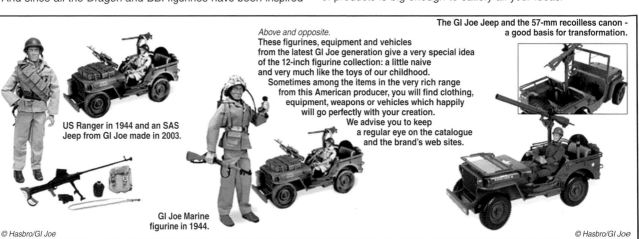

The GI Joe Jeep and the 57-mm recoilless canon - a good basis for transformation.

Above and opposite.
These figurines, equipment and vehicles from the latest GI Joe generation give a very special idea of the 12-inch figurine collection: a little naive and very much like the toys of our childhood. Sometimes among the items in the very rich range from this American producer, you will find clothing, equipment, weapons or vehicles which happily will go perfectly with your creation. We advise you to keep a regular eye on the catalogue and the brand's web sites.

US Ranger in 1944 and an SAS Jeep from GI Joe made in 2003.

GI Joe Marine figurine in 1944.

© Hasbro/GI Joe

© Hasbro/GI Joe

SIDESHOW

This American firm is known in the figurine world above all for its models inspired by successful films or television series: Frankenstein, Lon Chaney as a *Werewolf,* the *Monty Python Holy Grail,* Oliver Stone's *Platoon, Buffy the Vampire killer* and the Ian Fleming characters, *James Bond*, Sean Connery, Pierce Brosnan, Roger Moore, George Lazenby but Telly Savalas, Gert Froebe, Christopher Lee have also had the good fortune to be made by the *Sideshow* sculptors.

From a historical standpoint, the makers propose a very nice series of twenty or so figurines and panoplies on the American Civil War and the Wild West.

Much nearer to what interests us, over the last three years Sideshow has now brought out a very beautiful First World War collection.

Some of these accessories are very useful for creating certain figurines from the beginning of WWII. Moreover, the figurines' heads are so good and expressive that it would be criminal not to use them when creating your figurines.

The firm has even created three WWII heroes: *Hogan's Heroes.* These three characters were inspired from the famous television series.

The three figurines are Colonel Hogan, an 8th Air Force pilot; Colonel Klink, the Luftwaffe Colonel Commandant of the Stalag wearing a fur collared-coat; and Sergeant Schulz.

Here again the three figurines are also a mine of parts which can be used for conversions.

*Opposite, from left to right.
and top to bottom.*
The complete range of WWI figurines from *Sideshow*: **a French infantryman in 1917, a British Lewis Gunner, a Black Watch Grenadier, an Australian horseman on the Eastern Front, a Marine of the 5th Regiment in 1918, an American infantryman in 1917, a US Infantry Lieutenant, General Pershing, a Stosstruppe in 1917, a German infantryman, a flying officer, an infantryman in trench armour and an artillery lieutenant.**

Photographi © Sideshow

5

21st CENTURY TOYS

This other American firm is the oldest of the present big three and for the last ten years or so has brought out a range of figurines inspired by WWII, by the present day, by Hollywood phantasms about terrorism (*the Villains* series) or heroism (*America's Finest*).

Although the last two give more than their due to the SWAT intervention teams or to the Firemen, or even to the dastardly hooded terrorists, the other three are much closer to what we are after. The *Vietnam series* and give a complete range of infantrymen, specialists and members of special units having fought in the jungles of South-East Asia, in Afghanistan in the 80s or in Panama. They are mainly American, though there are some Soviets and some Viet-Cong and Vietnamese soldiers.

The series which interests us nowadays is very rich and can be separated into four categories: figurines, vehicles, displays and accessories.

On these two pages we have displayed the whole *WWII* range which is still available in France, in Europe or on the web (USA). Looking for the figurine you want can be a real assault course. The vehicles which are of the same scale as our figurines, although not legion, now make up an interesting choice. There is a Schwimmwagen, a PAK 40 anti-tank gun, two BMW 75s (one of which is Steve McQueen's from the *'Great Escape'*), a BMW sidecar, a Jeep, General Patton's Command Car, two versions of the

White Scout Car (a very muddy one from *21st century Toys* and one specially for the *Toys 'r Us* store chain brought out as brand new) and an M3A5 Stuart, available in three versions, Olive Drab, sand and two-tone camouflage. The makers have announced a GMC truck, a Half-Track and, although nobody believes it any longer, a German Panther tank.

Truly gold mines of spare parts, the blister packs containing accessories are on the whole given over to weapons: weapons for the allied special forces,.30 Browning water-cooled machine guns and.50s; US Marine Corps weapons, Sten guns, American bazookas of the first type with its rockets, German sub-machine guns, Wehrmacht rifles, weapons of the Axis powers (Japan, Italy and Germany), US flame throwers, Soviet weapons and a very beautiful blister pack containing the most characteristic weapons used in Indochina (and including the only MAT 49 in the history of the 12-inch figurine), a German inflatable raft.

The set displays use the same uniforms, equipment and weapons as the boxes of figurines though they are not so lavish. For example between the British Paratrooper in the box and the display, the purchaser will lose the haversack, the gasmask bag and a few other little accessories. If the uniforms and some equipment or weapons are indispensable, a great deal of the accessories look much more like toys than do the Chinese productions.

6

(Photographs © 21st century Toys)

THE ULTIMATE SOLDIER — U.S. MARINE JUNGLE FIGHTER

THE ULTIMATE SOLDIER — GERMAN MACHINE GUNNER

THE ULTIMATE SOLDIER — JAPANESE INFANTRY 1944

THE ULTIMATE SOLDIER — BRITISH 8TH ARMY

THE ULTIMATE SOLDIER — BRITISH COMMANDO

THE ULTIMATE SOLDIER — RUSSIAN INFANTRY (STALINGRAD)

(Photographis © 21st century Toys)

DRAGON series

(Photographs © Dragon)

In a few years, since 1999 in fact, Dragon has emerged as the undisputed leader for 12-inch figurine collectors.

With almost 500 items all series included, *Dragon* — the famous Hong Kong firm, which once upon a time used to specialise in plastic models — has become the unavoidable reference for anyone wanting to collect or work on 12-inch figurines.

Profusion, diversity, a coherent universe, the creators of the firm have won their bet: offering the most complete selection of WWII uniforms. Naturally, they have not made everything yet, but from experience we can confirm that you can realise several thousand figurines using the parts and uniforms already available.

We will only mention briefly the hundred or so modern references - from the Korean War to the capture of Baghdad, the SWAT Teams, the war against terrorism in Afghanistan, the Hong Kong Police, the SAS, the Coldstream Guards or the Secret Service bodyguards - and the less recent references (the 24th Foot Sergeant in South Africa, or the splendid knigths from the film *Timeline*) or figurines taken from recent films (Jean Reno in *Wazabi* or Will Smith in *Bad Boys II*).

The make's main production consists of WWII in general and the German Army in particular. However, for a bit more than two years now, Dragon's conceivers have not hesitated to open up their field of activities and they now produce more and more American, Soviet and British soldiers. We are greatly looking forward to and hoping for the moment when they bring out French, Japanese and Italian soldiers. With time, the quality of the accessories has improved exceptionally, as have the realism of the cloth and the way the different weapons and items of equipment work. This improvement in realism goes hand in hand with the variety of the themes they have chosen to produce, and as the different items appear the amateur discovers how rich the different outfits for each belligerent are.

Dragon is building up its different ranges into the most beautiful collection of figurines ever seen by bringing out ten new products every month. The crude and naïve appearance of the *GI Joe* figurines — the only range of products able to counter the Chinese steam-roller — and their accessories is all the more cruelly obvious. Naturally there are defects in the range. Certain accessories and even figurines are too fragile, too fine and undersized and this creates problems. On the other hand, there are some inventions which are worth mentioning: the rubber sleeves which can be slipped over the arms of figurines (who have rolled up sleeves) to hide the joints; or the very beautiful rubber legs for short-wearing soldiers which enable figurines under the tropics to be displayed with more realism. A quick and practical method for changing the heads without having to use a hairdryer still has to be found.

As well as its figurines, the make proposes an impressive array of accessories in blister packs which enable us to complete or improve this or that conversion. We must not forget to mention the very beautiful Kubelwagen they have brought out; it is Dragon's only sally into 'heavy' accessories.

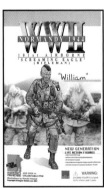

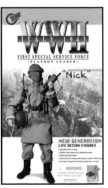

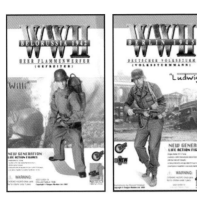

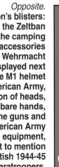

Opposite.
One of Dragon's blisters: the Zeltban and the camping accessories for the Wehrmacht are displayed next to the M1 helmet of the American Army, a collection of heads, gloved or bare hands, machine guns and American Army equipment, not to mention the British 1944-45 paratroopers.

9

GERMANY

Name	Description	Ref
Aloïs	Schütze, Fallschirm. Infanterie bataillon, 1938	70281
Peter Schmidt [8]	Schütze, Infantry, Blitzkrieg, 1939	70296
von Falkenburg [1]	Major, Parade Dress, Germany, 1939	70295
Konrad	Feldwebel, Fallschirmjäger, 1939-40	70145
Guderian [1]	General, Blitzkrieg, France, 1940	70231
Paul	Hauptscharführer, Verfügungstruppe 2.Standarte Germania, 1940	70123
Bruno	Schütze, Heer Infantry, France, 1940	70185
Galland [1]	Jageschwader 265 Schlagete, Battle of Britain, 1940	70…
Herbert	U-Boot Kapitän, Kriegsmarine, 1941	70…
Siegfried	Feldwebel, FJR 3., Crete 1941 (100th)	70…
Max [7]	Fallschirmjäger, Crete, 1941	70300
Max [3]	Fallschirmjäger, Crete, 1941 (avec parachute)	70300S
Klaus	Schütze, Wehrmacht Infantry, *Barbarossa,* 1941	70001
Hans	Feldwebel, Wehrmacht Infantry, *Barbarossa,* 1941	70002
Erich & Heinrich	German Infantrymen, Eastern Front 1941	70004
Hans	Feldwebel, Wehrmacht Infantry, Moscow, 1941*	70030
Karl	Feldgendarme, Leningrad, 1941	70003
Rommel	Feldmarshal, North Africa, 1942	70…
Egon	Squad Leader, DAK, North Africa, 1942	70112
Reinhardt	Gefreiter, DAK, 1942	70100
Ramcke [1]	General, Ramcke Brigade, Libya, 1942	70…
Leopold	Unterfeldwebel, *Ramcke Brigade,* Libya, 1942	70120
Felix	*Mathose,* Kriegsmarine Seaman, Dieppe 1942	70239
Georg	Stabbootman, Kriegsmarine, Dieppe, 1942	70195
Sep Kieffer	Hauptman, Nachrichten Abteilung 38, Smolensk 1942	70290
Gunther	Schütze, Gebirgsjäger, Caucasus, 1942	70070
Gunther [5]	Schütze, Gebirgsjäger, Caucasus, 1942 (in white)	70070S
Falkner	Zugfürher, 6. Armee, Kalach, 1942	70054
Elsa	German Nurse, DRK, Russia, 1942	70…
Willi [5]	Heer Flamenwerfer, Bielorussia, 1942	70196
Kurt	Feldwebel, 6. Armee, Stalingrad, 1942-43 *(JJSS)*	70049
Albert	Obergefreiter, Pz. Gren. Regt.1, Kzhev, 1942	70280
Marius	Gefreiter, 7. Panzer Division, Kursk, 1943	70274
Lang	Schweres Wurfgerät 41 & Rocket crew, Eastern Front, 1943	70200
Kurz	Obergrenadier, Rocket crew, Eastern front, 1943	70201
Max	NCO, SS-Pz. Grenadier, Zhitomir, 1943	70174
Arnold	13th Mountain Division *Andschar*	70156
Otto	Machine gunner, Grenadier, Kharkov, 1943	70010
Steiner	Feldwebel, Eastern Front, 1943	70…
Max [1]	Oberst, Project Adler, France, 1943	70210
Steiner [1]	Oberst, Project Adler, Great-Britain, 1943	70…
Werner	Gefreiter, Fallschirmjäger, Ukraine, 1943 (in white)	70110
Werner	Gefreiter, Fallschirmjäger, Ukraine, 1943 (in green) [5]	70110S
Uwe	Panzergrenadier, *GD* division, Karachev, 1943	70168
Udo	Landser, Ukraine, 1943	70153
Krieger	Fallschirmjäger, Italy, 1943-44	70122
Hugo	SS-Feldgendarme, Yugoslavia, 1944	70223
Baldur	Gefreiter, Panzer Aufklärungs-Abt.26, Salerno, 1943	70305
O. Skorzeny [1]	Hauptsturmführer, Gran Sasso, Italy, 1943	70…
Jurgen	Reichfürher, Italy 1944	70202
Gerhard	Unterfeldwebel, Panzerjäger, Crimea, 1944	70008
Horst & Blitz	Schütze, 3. Kavallerie division, Eastern Front, 1944	70020
Christian	Skijäger, winter 1944	70069
Ernst	Wehrmacht Sniper, Ukraine, 1944	70016
Volkmar	Panzergrenadier, *HG Division,* Anzio 1944	70157
M. Wittmann	Tiger Ace, Normandy, 1944	70…
Bobby Woll	Unterscharführer, Normandy 1944	70…
Woll & Wittmann [5]	Tiger Aces, Normandy, 1944	70… S
Marcus	MG 42 Gunner, HJ Division, Norrey-en-Bessin, 1944	70140
Viktor	Officer, *Panzer Lehr* Division, Normandy, 1944	70139
Milo	Grenadier, Normandy, 1944	70134
Rudi	Luftwaffe Field Division, Normandy, 1944	70189
Pieter	Unterfeldwebel, Fallschirmjäger, Normandy 1944	70083
Dieter	Infantryman with bicycle, France, 1944	70155
Marcus	*Hitler Jungend* division, 1944	70140
Hakon	NCO Panzergrenadier, 19. Regiment, Arnhem, 1944	70251
Karsten	Schütze, Panzergrenadier, Arnhem, 1944	70136
Meyer	Fallschirmjäger, 3. Division, Ardennes, 1944	70125
Lothar	Panzer-Grenadier, *LAH,* Kampfgruppe Hansen, Ardennes, 1944	70229
Edmund	Sturmbannführer, *Das Reich* Division, Ardennes, 1944	70170
Rudolf	Schütze, *Kampfgruppe Hansen,* Ardennes, 1944 **	70080
Jochen [1/7]	Kampfgruppe, Ardennes 1944	70142
Helmut	Pz. Grenadier, MG 42, *Das Reich Division,* Ardennes, 1944	70236
Hessler	Panzer Kampfgruppe Commander, Ardennes 1944	70…
Hessler [1]	Panzer Kampfgruppe Commander, Ardennes 1944 (Greatcoat)	70… S
Fritz	Obersturmfuhrer, *Wiking Division,* Poland, 1944	70007
Fritz	Obersturmfuhrer, *Wiking Division,* Poland, 1944 (in black)	70007S
Gerhard	Unterfeldwebel, Panzerjäger, East Prussia, 1944 (excl.)	70022
Erich Hartmann	Pilot, Luftwaffe (the blond Knight), 1944	70…
Krauer	Major (pilot), Luftwaffe, Prussia, 1944	70108
Eugen	Sanitätsgefreiter, 116. Pz. Division, Aachen, 1944	70293
Janos	Tank hunter, 51. Pz. Grenadier Rgt., Eastern Front, 1944	70299
Wolf	Schütze Grenadier, East Prussia, 1945	70009
Zanis	NCO 15. Waffen-SS gren. div., Dantzig, 1945	70219
Stefans	Grenadier, 15. Waffen. gren. Div., Dantzig, 1945	70011
Gross & Klein	Tank Hunters, Königsberg, 1945	70053
Alfred	Schütze, *LAH* Division, Aachen, 1945	70017
Franz	Grenadier, Pz. Division Totenkopf, Hungary, 1945	70308
Rolf Hoffman [1]	Panzer crewman, Fall. Pz. Div., Silesia, 1945	70…
Wilhelm	Schütze, German grenadier, Austria, 1945	70012
Hermann	Hauptscharführer, *Totenkopf* division, Budapest, 1945	70015
Volker	Schütze, *Totenkopf* division, Hungary, 1945	70018
Ansgar	Panzer-Grenadier, *Nordland* Division, Berlin 1945	70203
Ludwig	Volksturm, Berlin, 1945	70232
Johannes	Feldgendarme,	70117
Gustav & Kaiser	Feldgendarme and his dog,	70…
Wolfgang	Wehrmacht grenadier,	70009
Oskar Hodel	Panzer Unteroffizier, *Das Reich* Division,	70222
Kurt	Sturmbannführer *LAH,*	70130
Heinz	*Wiking* division,	70…
(?)	German Army Service female Officer [10]	70038

COMMONWEALTH		
Reggie	Private, 8th Army, North Africa, 1941-42	70190
Martin	Bren Gunner, 8th Army, North Africa, 1942	70240
Fred	Private, RTC, 7th Armoured Division, El Alamein 1942	73099
Fred 3	Private, RTC, 7th Armoured Division, El Alamein 1942	73099S
Liam	Private, Commonwealth Infantry, Western front, 1944-45	70173
Melvin	Private, Commonwealth Infantry, Western front, 1944-45	70204
Mark	Corporal, No 45 Commando, Royal Marines, Normandy 1944	70181
Ian	Paratrooper, 1st Airborne division, Arnhem, 1944	70175
Roy Urquhart 1	General, 1st Airborne division, Arnhem, 1944	70...

USRR		
Vassily	Tank Officer, Kursk, 1943	70210
Nikolaï	NCO, 38th Army, Kiev, 1943	70211
Dmitri	Seaman, Sewastopol, 1942	70207
Sasha	Rifleman, Poland, 1944	70206
Yuri	NCO, Infantryman, Stalingrad, 1942	70198
Boris	Sergeant, LMG Gunner, Ukraine, 1943-44	70301
Misha	Sniper, Stalingrad, 1944	70087
Natasha	Sniper, Stalingrad 1942	70...
Natasha	Sniper, Stalingrad 1942	70. S
Anna	NCO, Traffic Control Branch, Crimea 1944	70283
Vladimir	Scout, 1945	70285

UNITED STATES		
George Taylor	Pilot (P-40), USAAF, Pearl Harbor, 1941	70093
Ben Cole	Pilot, Flying Tigers, China, 1941	70094
George S. Patton 3	General, 1st Armored Corps, 1942 (*History Channel*)	73090
Skip	Captain, 8th Army Air Force, B-17 Pilot, England 1943	70138
NickCorrigan	Private, 1st SSF, Italy, 1943 (white dress)	70135S
Nick Corrigan	Private, 1st SSF, Italy, 1943	70135
Alan	Private, Sniper, 2nd Marines Div., Tarawa, 1943	70251
Pete	Technical Sergeant, 1st SSF, Italy, 1944	70092
Tak 9	Bar Gunner, 442nd regimental Combat team, Italy, 1944	70045
Yoshi 9	Rifleman, 442nd regimental Combat team, Italy, 1944	70...
Joe 1	Paratrooper, US Army Special Mission, France, 1944	70...
Lee 1	Major, US Army Special Mission, France, 1944	70141
Tom	Pathfinder 82nd Airborne, Normandy, 1944	70079
William	Rifleman, 101st Airtborne, Normandy 1944	70074
Charles 1	Colonel, 101st Airborne Divsion, Normandy 1944	70...
Miller	Captain, 2nd Rangers, Omaha Beach 1944	70005
Danny	Sergeant, 82nd Airborne Division, Normandy 1944	70...
"Sarge" 1 6	Squad Leader, ETO, 1944	70...
"Lieutenant" 1	1st Lieutenant, Infantry Division, ETO, 1944	70...
King Company 1	"Sarge" & Lieutenant, Squad leaders, ETO, 1944	70...
Nagashima	Sergeant, 100th Infantry Battailon, Italie, 1944	70292
Dave	Sergeant, 1st infantry Division, Normandy, 1944	70021
Scott	Rifleman, 4th Infantry Division, France 1944	70023
Scott	Rifleman, 4th Infantry Division, France 1944 (w. poncho)	70023S
Mac 6	Staff Sergeant, 3rd Armoured Division, France, 1944	70180 1
Craig 6	1st Lieutenant, 9th Infantry Division, France, 1944	70212
O. Bradley	Lieutenant General, 12th Army Group, France 1944	70239
Sean	BAR gunner, 9th Infantry Division, France, 1944	70...
"Big" Joe 1	Master Sergeant, 35th Infantry Division, France 1944	70...
Kelly 1	Private, 35th Infantry Division, France 1944	70...
Bud 6	Rifleman, 4th Infantry Division, France 1944	70213
Lou 6	Army MP, 8th Infantry Division, Britanny, 1944	70279
Wiley 6	BAR Gunner, 7th Armored Division, Ardennes, 1944	70171
William 1	Colonel, 1st Infantry Division, POW, Germany, 1944	70128
Roscoe	Private, 630th tank destroyer	70152
"Doc" Peterson 6	Infirmier, 94th Infantry Division, Moselle, 1945	70245
Peck & Hunt 6	Machine Gun team, 77th Inf. Division, Guam, 1944	70214
Jeb 6	BAR Gunner, 17th Airborne division, Varsity, 1945	70159
Jeb 6	BAR Gunner, 17th Airborne division, Varsity, 1945	70159S
Joe Enders 4	Corporal, USMC, Pacific, 1944	73069
Ox Henderson 4	Corporal, USMC, Pacific, 1944	73070
Ben Yahzee 4	Radio Operator, USMC, Pacific, 1944	73071
Sonny	Flamethrower, USMC, Iwo Jima, 1945	70169
Barney	« Bunker Buster », 4th Division USMC, Iwo-Jima, 1945	70235
Zeke	Rifleman, USMC, Iwo Jima, 1945	70197
	BAR Gunner, USMC, Iwo Jima 1945	70...

1. Figurines with numbered cards realised exclusively for *Cyber Hobby*.
2. Figurines realised exclusively for *JJSS*.
3. Figurines stamped *History Channel*, Great leaders in WWII matters.
4. Figurines taken from the John Woo film *Windtalkers*.
5. Special *Dragon series* with added elements or colour changes.
6. 'Road to victory' Series.
7. A Figurine from one of *Dragon's* anniversary commemorative series.
8. A new series of highly detailed figurines from Dragon called *'Soldat'* (Soldier).
9. Series realised for a Hong Kong toy shop chain.
10. Figurine presented in the 2000 catalogue and never produced.

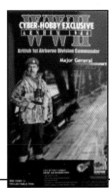

Preceding page, top.
A selection of *Dragon* boxes from the first references.

Opposite and below.
Some of the *Dragon* Limited runs for *Cyber Hobby*.
(Photos Dragon and Cyber Hobby).

BLUE BOX INTERNATIONAL

The last arrival on the market in 2000, *Blue Box International* is a Chinese firm which is well-established in the USA. Its '*Elite Forces WWII*', '*Elite Force*', '*Aviators*' and '*Vilains*' series provide a still limited though very promising range.

The make has started competing with Dragon by bringing out modern figurines (SAS, SEALs, SWAT, Delta Forces, etc.) with magnificent uniforms and accessories; but at the beginning the characters were a bit 'light', the selling tack being the weapons, the metal helmets and the very competitive price.

Today, *BBI* has brought out an impressive modern range with more than forty figurines (more or less available) and a WWII range which complements and even competes with *Dragon*. As you will see later in this book, mixing parts from the two top makes is frequent and even recommended.

For its WWII figurines, *BBI* has given up its idea of 'metal weapons' as they were unable to realise them finely enough, but has maintained the idea of the 'heavy' metal helmet. This has certainly meant more realism but it does also mean that the figurine can topple over when it is finished. Moreover, it has to be admitted that the general shape of the American helmet, for example, has been botched and that it can only be used with a Marine Corps cover from… *Dragon*.

Apart from this particular problem, as a general rule, *BBI* show more inventiveness and attention to small details than others.

To convince yourself of this you only have to take the American Paratrooper, the English Commando in Libya or the British Paratrooper. Each *BBI* box is a real Ali Baba's cavern full of accessories, like a compass, a penknife, maps etc. With it latest productions, *Dragon* has launched itself in this direction and no longer hesitates to fill up its boxes and make the collectors very happy indeed.

The *BBI* figurines are still difficult to evaluate. Although the faces are more and more realistic, and are beyond the canon imposed for 'dolls', the bodies are not easy to move. Although *BBI* has made an effort with the joints in the most recent products, they are still not very realistic and the collector has to have a lot of imagination and fill in the hollows of the thorax or the shoulder blades. Likewise, the wrist joint is practical but is hardly credible once the uniform is worn.

As a general rule, *BBI* characters are anatomically strange: everything is hollows and bumps, the hands are oversized and the feet undersized but the heads ands faces are absolutely realistic. Whatever the problem may be, *BBI* figurines are just as essential to your collection as Dragon's are.

Although there are not a lot of them at the present moment, the accessories are very beautiful. There are parachute ensembles for Luftwaffe, RAF, USAAF pilots and the two types of parachutes used in Normandy or during *Operation Varsity*. The RAF seat parachu-

te is very nice indeed and the strap fastening system is an exact replica of the original.

In 2002, the brand brought out four-piece obstacles found on the Normandy beeches, sandbags made of jute and barbed wire to be assembled barb by barb. The three blister packs are very beautiful and enable you to imagine some nice, simple little scenes.

Opposite left.
The famous beach obstacles, to be assembled: these are very realistic and there are two in a box. There are also four sandbags per blister pack and four rolls of barbed wire in each reference.

Opposite, right.
The LRDG officer a great succees in the *BBI*'s range.

THE *ELITE FORCE - SECOND WORLD WAR RANGE* FROM *BLUE BOX INTERNATIONAL*   *(Photographs BBI and A&C)*

	GERMANY				
Max	Fallshirmjäger, Crète, 1941		Neil Williams	Sergeant, 6th Airborne Division, Normandy, 1944	21100
Otto Schulz	Oberleutnant, Luftwaffe, Libya, 1942		Harry Sinclair	Sergent, servant de PIAT, Burma, 1944	21172
Rudi Kessling	Obergefreiter, Gebirgsjäger, Deustche Afrika Korps, 1942	21137	Paddy Ryan	Corporal, infanterie australienne, Burma, 1944	21171
Johan Jergens	Oberfeldwebel, Deustche Afrika Korps, 1942	21154		UNITED STAES	
Ernst Wagner	Major, Pilote, Luftwaffe, germany, 1944	21093	Doc Miller	Lieutenant, pilote de P-40, Pearl Harbor, 1941	34333
Franz Haas	Artilleur, 21. Panzer Division, Normandy 1944	21065	Dusty Rhodes	Sergeant, US Marine Corps, Pacific Ocean, 1944	21084
	Pz. Gren., 12. SS-Panzer Division, Normandy 1944		Hoppy Bell	Sergent, 5th Rangers Battalion, Normandy, 1944	
Dieter Voss	Gefreiter, Panzer Grenadier, Ardennes 1944	21101	Budd Norris	Caporal, 101st Airborne Division, France, 1944	21066
	COMMONWEALTH		Red Parker	Caporal, 2nd infantry Division, France, 1944	
Donald Moore	Flight Lieutenant, Royal Air Force, Libya, 1942		Wil Bailey	Infirmier, 101st Airborne Division, Operation *Varsity*, 1945	
Peter Keyes	Bren Gunner, Commando, Libya, 1942		Chuck Hayes	Lieutenant, 1st infantry Division, Germany, 1945	
Douglas Caldwell	Captain, Long Range Desert Group, Libya, 1942			JAPAN	
	Wing Commander, Royal Air Force, England, 1943		Sakae	Lieutenant, Japanese Navy, pilot, Pearl Harbor 1941	34332
Robert James	Private, N° 2 Commando, Normandy, 1944		Saburo Nakagawa	Officer, Infanterie, Pacific Ocean, 1943	21173
			Yamamoto Ichiro	Infantryman, Japanese Navy, Pacific Ocean, 1943	21085

BASIC EQUIPMENT

1. ASSEMBLY

In order to work correctly on 12 inch figurines one has to have basic tooling which in fact is not very different from the ordinary model-maker's. First get together a set of *X-Acto* knives or cutters (balsa knives) for slicing and trimming if needed; flat files —rat tails or round — of different sizes and lengths.

For rubbing, emery paper nail files, also of different sizes are recommended as is abrasive car bodywork glass paper, double or even triple zero.

Sets of tweezers and pliers are indispensable for holding, shaping or for simply holding and pulling things like straps and other belt-like things.

Useful but not indispensable things to have are: punches, lengths of metal (wire) to shape into buckles and rings, and small vices. In the less-model-making-and-more-needlework domain, you will need a small pair of sewing scissors, needles of different diameters and a thimble if you have fragile fingers.

2. STICKING

Five types of glue can be used. The usual plastic glues in the case of broken parts or parts which have to be added; the cyanoacrylate glues for certain metal or cloth parts if you do not want

With these characters, both *Dragon* and *BBI*, representing soldiers from the 8th Army in Libya, one can appreciate the two makers' different approach when it comes to the finish of the cloth and the accessories. We will not dwell on the knobbly knees of *BBI*'s LRDG Lieutenant on the right.

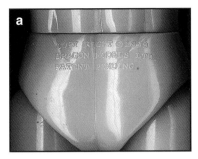

a

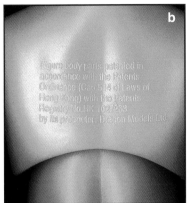

b

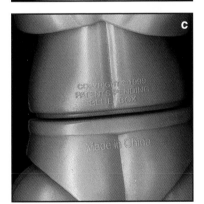

c

d

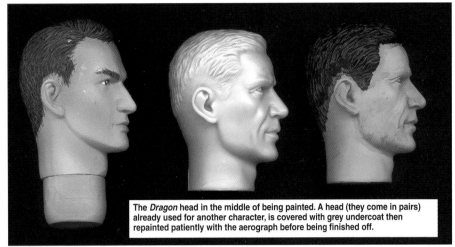

The *Dragon* head in the middle of being painted. A head (they come in pairs) already used for another character, is covered with grey undercoat then repainted patiently with the aerograph before being finished off.

Above: from right to left.
The *BBI* head mounted on a rotating neck, itself mounted on the body ball and socket joint. The *Dragon* head which is mounted more simply turns around on an axis mounted on the neck which is articulated to the body. Although this is more natural it is impossible to dismantle it without the help of a hair dryer and pliers.

Opposite from top to bottom.
The names given to the models and the copyright of the principal types of *Dragon* figurine in 1999 (a) and the revolution in 2000 (b) and *BBI* in 1999 (c) and 2002 (d).

The way *Dragon* hands have evolved:
1. BBI gloved hands. The wrist goes into the glove. The long stalk which can be seen just sticking out is mounted on a ball and socket joint with very little travel. The hand assembly is very fragile.
2. Gloved hands from *Dragon*, second type. The fingers are supple without being soft and can be moved. The wrist turns and the joint is identical to that of the bare hands. The assembly is more solid. In 2a (cut out) and 2b (holes), the possible articulations.
3. *Dragon* hands, 2nd type.
4. *BBI* hands mounted on joints which came out in 2002.
5. *BBI* hands, first type (1999). The joint is simple but the movement scarcely natural.
6. Comparison between *Dragon* hands, 2nd Type (6a) and first type (6b) which are too big. The third type is comparable to the gloved hands seen in 2.

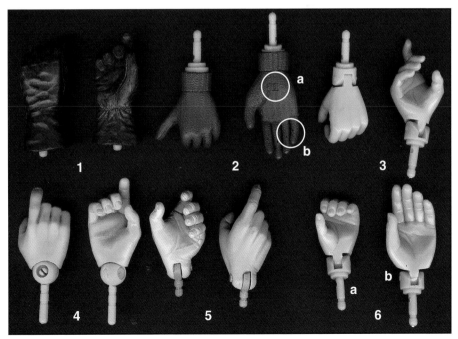

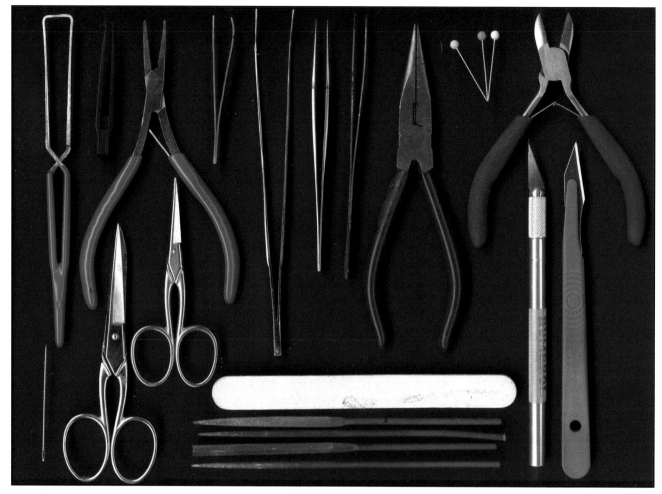

to use glue for cloth which is less easy to use. Two-component glue for plastic can be useful in the case of parts which have to be repaired but which will not be moving a great deal.

Paste can also be useful with modifications using cloth or cardboard. It can be useful also for dirtying.

3. COLOURING

Generally the colours and shades of the uniforms and the equipment are good and normally there is nothing to be done here.

Sometimes, it may be necessary to repaint a grenade or the iron of a spade; you'll have to get together some paints: acrylic (*Prince August* or *Games Workshop*), spirit (*Humbrol*) or oil (*Talens Rembrandt* or *Lefranc Bourgeois*). Classic solvents, siccatives and other delayers can turn out to be useful. We shall see later when to use or not such and such a shade or type of paint.

Paints for use on cloth (*Pebeo Setacolor*), *equaline* or acrylic inks (*Games Workshop*, *Colorex Technics*) may be used in certain conditions and for very precise uses.

Branded oil pastels *Rembrandt* are used to dirty and age clothing and equipment. Our photo shows a selection of indispen-

The tools which are essential for transforming or improving large sized figurines: pliers, tweezers, cutter (balsa knife), knife, sewing scissors, cutting pliers, flat files, 'rat's tails', emery paper, needles and pins.

sable pastels. Your talents where colours are concerned will no doubt enable you to find other shades which are more adapted to your needs.

4. CLOTH AND FELT

Felt and cloth of different colours and thicknesses are to be used for small changes or to vary the shades and the material of existing items of clothing (armbands, scarves, tarbooshes, handkerchiefs, shoulder flap loops, helmet covers, etc.). Recovering bits and pieces is the first and only real source of supply. Felt is sold in packets or in self-adhesive rolls.

Here are a few simple tips for transforming and improving your figurines which only need a minimum of time or handling. It is possible to make your figurine realistic or life-like in a little less than three hours using means and technical know-how which will not put a novice off.

5. 'FATTENING'

This operation is not indispensable but it will add a realistic note to all your figurines. The 12-inch figurines tend to look starved, with flat buttocks, thin thighs and chickenleg-like calves. These are the three areas which have to be 'fattened'

Be careful not to overdo it: the risks of not being able to get the clothes on or of getting the volume out of proportion are quite real. Polyurethane foam is the easiest substance to handle. You can cut it to the sizes you want and add extra layers. Its consistence is soft and does not interfere very much with wearing clothes and adapts to the trousers and the leggings.

However, be careful and carry out trial runs using adhesive tape to hold it in place and to find the right thickness and place; it is difficult to reposition the buttocks once they have been stuck with cyanoalicrate glue.

The three photographs opposite show three examples among a host of solutions.

6. IMPROVING THE HANDS

Dragon hands for instance are fine and rather well done but

shine too much and really look too much like plastic… which they are! *BBI* hands are rather beautiful though sometimes a little out of proportion and are more realistic. Unfortunately the system for attaching them is not the same and it is almost impossible to attach the hands of one make's model onto another's. Moreover I find that the BBI joint is not very aesthetic and almost impossible to hide. It is therefore necessary to improve the hands.

THREE SOLUTIONS: THE FASTEST TO THE LONGEST

The first consists of putting a wash of hazel paint in the cracks, the folds and the articulations of both hands with a fine brush. Dull with a couple of rapid wipes with pink, orange, brown and black oil pastel. Fix with hair fixative. This technique dulls and dirties the hands. About ten minutes for one hand.

The second means painting the hands with Humbrol paint and wiping a skin-coloured with brown wash into the hollows; and then

The two-component plastic glues, polystyrene, araldite, for cloth; inks, paints for cloth, acrylic paint for the aerograph or not, pastels, eraser: everything to make things better.

Above.
Several faces at different stages of camouflage. The first, on the left is that of the German sharpshooter at Stalingrad, an 'out-of-the-box' face. The following which strangely resembles Russel Crowe's face, has been wiped with black oil pastel to give it the smoke of fighting. The following two have been reworked according to model makers' methods, shadows, light and scars, etc.

Dragon legs — covered with rubber sleeves to hide the joints — have been repainted with ochre, brown and orange Rembrandt pastels. The strips on the ankles, the long brown socks and the boots have been worked over in the same manner. The only difference between the legs and the clothing is in the way the pastel has been fixed... with hair spray.

dry-brushing the basic colour, lightened on the relief parts. If you do not like using spirit paints you can use acrylic paints. Hardly more than twenty minutes with the acrylic paints.

The third consists of repainting the hands with the techniques used by the figurine makers, with oil or acrylic paints. We advise painting the hands first with an aerograph. In this case, we use the basic shades from *Games Workshop*: Dwarf skin, elf skin or tanned skin, diluted. Paint over several times. For the details use either oil or acrylic.

18

The hands may have to be aged and dirtied: we recommend a wash of much diluted oil or acrylic paint. Our photos give you an idea of the three techniques.

7. FACES

Naturally you can repaint all the faces, but in the end, with the exception of the very first Dragon or BBI productions, the faces are realistic.

One has to improve them by dry-brushing the hair or highlighting the bags under the eyes, or dirtying different parts of the face using pastels rubbed with a cloth, or a black or brown wash.

At 1/6th scale, two day's stubble measures less than 1 mm and can be simulated with a dark grey shadow or a bluish grey for brown haired people, wiped over the chin or the cheeks with the help of a sponge, or a thin veil with the aerograph (pure black looks too artificial).

8. AGEING CLOTHES

This stage will make all the difference between a straight-out-of-the-box model with its artificial look and a figurine which has been around a bit. From the slightly creased jacket to the trousers stiff with mud, anything is possible.

— Pastels.

The easiest and the quickest method — and we have used it several times in the course of this book — very simply consists rubbing the tops of the folds and seams with white oil pastel. The inside of these folds are shaded with a darker colour.

The next step consists of softening these colours by rubbing the cloth with a rag, then with fine car bodywork emery paper. These successive operations soften the tones and get the colour to penetrate into the weave of the cloth, wearing the clothes naturally.

— Washes.

With the help of a concoction of tea, normal or herbal, you can taint in depth without changing the basic colours. Thus you can create a more or less light veil, depending on the time the item has been left to soak. Thus for certain 'brown' teas, you can taint the uniforms of the Heer or the Waffen-SS naturally.

Washes with very diluted oil paints will give brown, yellow, greenish, ochre veils depending on the types of paints used and the type of cloth. Very diluted (with lighter fuel) spirit paints (of the *Humbrol* type) give a matter tone than other techniques.

— Abrasives.

With different grain emery paper and depending on the number of 'rubs' and the amount of pressure, you can wear out clothes, make holes in the cloth, all very naturally. Triple zero is the type of Emery paper which we normally use.

— Micro painting.

As for armoured vehicle, plane or figurine models, you can stain paint and repaint clothes and items of equipment. Use your own techniques, if you are a model-maker. For the others we can show you some of the basic techniques.

— Thick mud stains can be applied using Humbrol paint directly without diluting it with spirit.

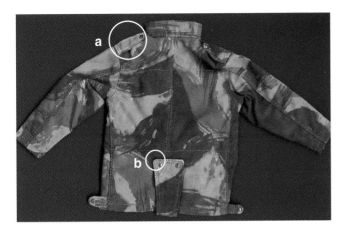

The *Dragon* Denison Smock has been repainted using special *Prince August* acrylic paint for aerographs and *Pebeo Colorex Technic* acrylic inks. In a and b the original colours were much too pale.

— **Finer stains** are painted directly with acrylic paints or applied with oil pastels.

— **Dust and snow** are applied using a more or less light halo of aerograph-applied acrylic paint.

— **Petrol and oil stains** can be made with oil paints, more or less diluted with turpentine.

Powdered pastels, sprinkled on the clothes before being very lightly covered with glue paste or matt varnish give excellent muddy and dusty crusts.

The choice of shades is infinite. 'Crusts' can be created using grass and sand, etc., and a variety of substances sold in graphic art shops. Beware: some of these supports are white or colourless.

You can mix all these techniques and materials in order to get what you want, the end result.

REPAINTING CLOTHES

Re-tinting or rather repainting clothes is always possible as long as you do not want to change white into black. Change pale into dark colours where possible or by using several very much diluted layers.

Cloth paints are excellent as they do not make the cloth too rigid or too brittle; however, there is not a great variety of colours. There is a greater choice with acrylic paints, but they tend to make the clothing brittle.

To reduce this effect, which can have disastrous effects, as much as possible, you have to work with greatly diluted paints and by applying several layers. Spirit paints can be very practical as long as they are really diluted, but with lighter fuel.

Finally, moderately diluted acrylic inks can also turn out to be very useful. It was by mixing the acrylic shades (paints and inks) that we painted the Denison Smock of the Dragon Paratrooper.

All the various techniques which we have sketched out can also be used on cloth or canvas equipment.

The equipment (sometimes made out of plastic) and the wea-pons (always made of plastic) must be aged and treated like a figurine or a model, with interplay of light and shadows, washes and dry-brushing.

The metal of the weapons can be repainted matt black and dry-brushed with acrylic silver or even better, *Metal bolter* or metal, paint.

MAKING INSIGNIA

Most of WWII soldiers wore unit insignia, rank markings or speciality badges. If you do not want to use the ones provided by the makers of your figurine or if you do not have access to those sold by certain American specialists, we advise you to make them yourself.

For this all you need is to have a scanner and a colour printer. You scan the insignia which you want you men to wear. You reduce them to the right size (the good books give the dimensions of the original insignia), i.e. you divide the sides by 6 and you print them on a self-adhesive sheet which you can get in shops selling paper for printers. Print a whole sheet to get a good return.

Then you cut the insignia out with sewing scissors, give them a little touch of paint with the right colour on the thickness of the paper and then stick it with cloth or cyanoacrilate glue. The thickness thus obtained is perfect.

In the following pages, you will discover all these techniques applied to figurines.

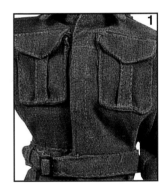

1 and 3. A British battledress and a khaki drill shirt from the 8th Army have been aged mainly by using white (pure white and off white) and ochre pastels from Rembrandt on the folds and the seams; the darker pastels were used in the hollows and under the seams. Everything was then rubbed down lightly with emery paper.

2. American combat dress trousers worn out by using Emery paper mainly. The lower angle of the pocket has been rubbed down so as to wear a hole in it.

12. SS-Panzer Division, Hitlerjugend in Normandy
(Diorama created by Claude Messmer. Action figures Dragon, BMW R75 Ultimate Soldier /21st Century Toys)

THE FRENCH

Tirailleur, 3rd Regiment, Algerian Tirailleurs, 3rd Algerian division, Italy 1944

(RR)

Up to now there are no 1: 6 figurines of French WWII soldiers. There exist a 1916 *"Poilu"* and a Legionary from the 90s in Kosovo and between them: nothing!

This is why we decided to present you with these three fighters from Eternal France.

First of all we made up an Algerian Tirailleur — of European origin as there was no figurine which could credibly represent a North-African — from the French Expeditionary Corps in Italy.

Without French equipment, or almost, and wishing to give you some simple ideas, we were obliged to cheat a bit and realise figurines with mixed up uniforms. Thus our Tirailleur is a Dragon figurine and is wearing the shirt and trousers of an American infantryman. His boots are of the same make. The gaiters are parts from the first *BBI* plastic models.

The.30 ammunition magazine belt comes from the *BBI* Marine. To attach the *Dragon* suspenders belts it was necessary to pierce six little holes in the belt. The first two in front between the first and second pouches (on each side of course); the other two between the third and the fourth pouches (still on each side); and the last two behind the last pouch of each row.

The water flask, its holder and the wire cutters and their sheath are from *BBI*. The bayonet and its sheath attached with hooks to the belt are *Dragon* accessories. The Springfield rifle which was widely distributed to the French forces equipped by the Americans comes from the *Sideshow* box of the Marine, 5th Regiment in 1918.

The only specifically French parts come from the horizon blue French infantryman by Sideshow.

The helmet, a 1916 model, has been covered by a cloth helmet cover cut out from a helmet cover for US Marine Corps figurines from *Dragon*. We repainted it Khaki (2/3 *Prince August* Olive Drab and 1/3 brown of the same make). The helmet cover is glued into the correct shape.

The bag comes from the 1916 *"Poilu"* and has been filled with silk paper to give it some volume. The walking stick which is so often seen on period photographs has been carved out of a wooden skewer and then painted.

Resistance Fighter, Forces Françaises de l'Intérieur (FFI), Paris, August 1944

We admit that making this figurine gave us a lot of pleasure. Starting from period photographs and a slightly over-Hollywoodian vision of the Resistance movement, we started on our resistance fighter.

The character is the *Sideshow* 1918 French infantryman. We made him a good French beret from an old one produced three years ago for the Royal Marines by *BBI*. Reshaped, repainted and stuck onto the character, it gives the right effect.

The white shirt is taken from the MiG pilot by *BBI*. This article has a wide collar which enabled us to place it over the collar of the jacket, a typical arrangement for men's fashion in the 1940s.

The jacket is from the 1999 *Dragon* Secret Agents. The brown trousers come from one of *Dragon's* American boxes. The boots are the same as those of the infantryman mentioned above. The armband was cut from a piece of cloth and really tied around the arm.

The letters FFI have been gauchely hand-painted with *Games Workshop* black ink. The Sten Mk II comes from the beautiful *21st century Toys* pack which contains several models of this weapon. The belt, the pistol holster and its contents, a splendid P-38 and the two stick grenades are «war-prizes» taken from one of the very many *Dragon* boxes given over to the German Army. In the end it was not making this particular model which caused us the most trouble.

The tarboosh was cut out of a piece of ochre cloth and tied around the neck of our legionary.

The model 35 kepi is a pure creation, made from strong cardboard, covered with two pieces of crude cloth (one for the circumference and the other for the height), and whitened with pastel.

The fake black chinstrap and the two

little buttons were made from plastic card. The peak was made out of cardboard painted black. The dimensions and the proportions have been taken from the plates gathered together and commented on by François Vauvillier in *'Les Uniformes de l'Armée Française 1939-40'* (French Army Uniforms 1939-40), essential reading.

(RR)

Legionary, 13th DBLE, Bir Hakeim 1942

If we mixed French and American items for our Tirailleur, this time they were French and English.

The basic figurine is Dragon's *"Reggie"*, a Bren Gunner in the 8th Army. From this we kept the short-sleeved khaki drill shirt, the boots and the puttees (the straps wrapped around the calves common to English infantrymen of the period) and the long brown socks.

The first type of shorts issued to the English Army and worn by our legionary could reach down to mid calf or, as here, be pulled up with the aid of little cotton straps; the shorts come from *BBI*'s English North African Commando.

This article of clothing was typical of the period.

The French equipment comes from *Sideshow's* WWI French Infantryman: the 1903-14 belt, the 1892-1914 suspender belts, the three 1916-model cartridge pouches (two in front and one behind), the two-litre 1935-model water bottle and the tan-coloured (*cachou*) cloth haversack.

The water bottle was repainted in khaki as the part's original horizon blue was not appropriate for the desert.

THE JAPANESE

This Japanese officer is one of *BBI*'s best creations to date. The sculptor has caught the traits of the archetypal Asiatic face. This was not the case with the figurine on the next page and in order to present this character, we had to use "*Tak*", the *Dragon* BAR Gunner of the 442nd Combat Group whose face was much more Asiatic than the figurine provided by *BBI*. However that may be, our officer is correctly accoutred with all the parts provided, from the jacket and the trousers of the Uniform model 98 to the complex assembly of belts and straps used by the Japanese officer.

This way of carrying equipment, saltire-wise (i.e. crossed straps over the shoulders) was rather close to the French idea of what an officer's equipment should be. The sabre-belt was worn under the jacket. The sabre ring could be attached higher up on the belt by means of a ring and a hook, when the officer was marching.

The finish of the leather and the blade of the sabre are of a very high standard. Of course everything 'works' and can be opened. The only hitch is in the way the golden sabre knot has been rendered.

Junior Officer Rank Insignia (Collar markings)

Captain

1st Lieutenant

2nd lieutenant

BBI and 21st Century are the only makers who have brought out a figurine of a Japanese soldier. He is a Fusilier of the Japanese Navy Infantry in 1942. The uniform is the 98 model introduced in 1938. The helmet is the 92 model (1932) made of steel, covered with flannelette cloth upon which has been stitched the Navy anchor on a little circle of cloth the same colour as the uniform. The typically complex system of chinstrap has been very well rendered here. The Infantryman in the *BBI* box also has a cloth campaign hat to which has been added a three-piece neckcloth with its little tightening cord at the back.

The jacket of the uniform made here of cotton in its tropical version includes the bayonet's little fixing strap on the left-hand side. The five metal buttons have been struck with the Navy anchor and cherry leaf. The trouser-breeches are covered with flannelette strips whose long tightening cords have been arranged X-wise, Japanese-style; it took several attempts to tighten the strips around the legs of our Infantryman before getting the right effect since each successive thickness of the trousers and the boots created problems.

The reproduction of the boots has been done quite well and after a bit of reworking they can open up other possibilities for figurines in other armies.

The belt and the three leather cartridge pouches (two in front, one behind) conform to the original items and open; be careful however as the openings are rather fragile. The water bottle and its strap are well and truly those of the Navy, which are not to be confused with the much better known Army model 93. The lightened haversack, which is not the one that contains the gas mask, is made of cloth. The model 38 Arisaka Rifle dates back to 1906 and had the smallest calibre of WWII: 6.5 mm.

The clothes and equipment have been dirtied and made to look worn with pastel and emery paper.

THE RED ARMY

NKVD Sharpshooter, Stalingrad, 1942-43

Apart from the two references from *21st Century Toys*, only *Dragon*, the Chinese firm, has brought out any Russian soldiers.

The range of products is now sufficiently varied to permit a great deal of transformations. In these pages we give suggestions for slightly improved straight-out-of-the box models, but this catalogue should enable you to undertake the figurines that tempt you.

Dragon seems to be making up for lost time, and has been bringing out at least one Soviet soldier every three months for the last two years now.

The sharpshooter, the first of all these characters is one of the oldest. Misha is part of the double box *'Duel at Stalingrad'*, inspired by the film of the same name by Jean-Jacques Annaud. Our man is a member of the NKVD, indicated by the colour of the piping on his collar board: dark red.

He is wearing the famous *Shapka-Ushanka*, a fleece-lined *Telogreika* jacket, model 1935 trousers, hobnailed boots and puttees (these last two items are moulded in one piece).

Under the jacket, Misha is wearing a *Gymnastiorka* shirt. The tent-cloth (worn saltire-wise), a belt, two model 1930 cartridge pouches and a water bottle make up the equipment for our man. The rifle, a Mosin-Nagant 1891-30 is fitted with telescopic sights. As in the film, the sharpshooter can be 'camouflaged' with his tent cloth.

Sailor, Black Sea Fleet, Sebastopol, 1943

Dmitri the Sailor or *Krasnoflotets* (literally 'the red sailor') is one of the most exotic and beautiful figurines produced by *Dragon*.

The flat hat, inseparable from the Russian sailor's silhouette, has been embellished with the long ribbon on which is inscribed in Cyrillic script *'Black Sea Fleet'*; it can be replaced by a second one supplied with the box.

The presence of a dark blue smock (*Flanelevka*) worn over the legendary blue and white striped shirt, shows that our sailor has put his winter gear on.

In the factory, the smock has had

a red star - in fact an indication of rank- thermo stuck on the right sleeve.

The sailor is wearing a regulation belt with an anchor and a star on the plate; this fastens more easily than the ones supplied by the producers for the Russian Army.

Two types of cartridge pouches have been put on to the belt: in front, the classic vulcanised (war production) cloth 1930 models; behind, the Imperial 1893 model cartridge pouch which was longer; this

Sharpshooter, Ukraine 1944

The *Dragon* box also contains a bag for the BN gas mask and two Model 1933 hand grenades.

Our woman sharpshooter, the first Soviet box from *Dragon*, is called *Svetlana*. She is available in two versions: with moulded (as in our photograph) or flowing nylon hair. In our opinion, the first is more realistic since it does not make her look like a *Barbie Doll*.

Our sharpshooter is equipped like Misha but instead of the fleece-lined jacket, she has been given a two piece irreversible camouflage suit with large wavy green and brown patches.

The hood is functional but as with all clothing items using cords, there is a little bit of cutting and fixing to be done.

has to be painted matt. The aluminium flask in its cloth cover is attached by means of a flap to the belt over his right hip. The little flap holding the cover to the flask is to be glued and the ends of the cords cut once the whole has been tightened. Once this has been done, singe the two ends of cord with a lighter to stop them splaying, then tint them to cover the burn marks.

The sailor is wearing two ammunition belts for the Maxim Machine Gun over his shoulders. This feature of fighting Soviet sailors has been well captured by the maker. From a practical standpoint, each man carried a least one belt, which considerably increased the ammunition supplies of the units of the fleet engaged in the fighting… and when one knows that the theoretically each infantry battalion was supplied with fifteen machine guns. The navy blue trousers have a big flap. This was particular to the sailors as it prevented them, apparently, from getting their flies and buttons caught in the shrouding. In his regulation boots, our sailor has slipped the bayonet from his weapon; this is a semi-automatic Tokarev 7.62 which was supplied in great numbers to the Navy. It was an excellent weapon although it was complex and complicated to service. It was handed out to experienced NCOs and sailors who were more careful and less engaged in the harsh land fighting.

27

Infantryman, the Battle for Moscow, 1941

This character, whom we have rather arbitrarily put in front of Moscow defending it against the invading German troops, can serve as an illustration for any Russian combatant for the four years of the war. He can be considered as typical.

Our *Dragon* figurine has not been changed or aged; it is a typical 'straight out of the box', ready for all sorts of transformations.

The soldier is wearing the 1940-model *Shapka-Ushanka* made of fleece-lined cloth. The fur on the original, as on the model, is synthetic.

This headgear which can be placed under a helmet on another figurine has been copied by all countries or almost and is ideal for very cold regions. The ear flaps fold down, in which case we advise cutting the cords.

The red enamel star pinned on to the front of the hat can be painted khaki in accordance with the regulations for combat dress.

The padded jacket is a Model 1941 *Telogreika*. The model produced by *Dragon* is not the regulation one, but one of the numerous versions made by the Red Army.

The initial model fastened further to the right and did not have straps on the wrists. The trousers were cut from the same material as the jacket, but they were much less common than the jacket.

The leather belt is the same as was worn during WWI. *Dragon* belts do not all fasten in the same way.

The buckle and the tongue here are token; to replace them, two studs are in fact inserted into two holes on the inside of each end of the belt; a loop holds the two ends fast.

This system does not always work very well.

The leather boots have been very well reproduced but they would be more realistic if they were more shapeless.

The equipment consists of a simple round sheath in strong khaki cloth containing one spare PPSH 41 machine pistol magazine (more than 5 million 1941-model 7.62 mm Shopagins were produced).

As our character is only wearing a shirt under the jacket, a scarf can be added and a pair of gloved hands can be found for him, which would make the whole more realistic.

Infantryman, Polish Front, 1944

This infantryman is also a 'straight-out-of-the-box' *Dragon* figurine and the details have only been slightly improved particularly concerning the fittings and the wear and tear of these items of clothing and equipment. Our man is wearing a *Pilotka* (forage cap) recovered from the *Dragon* 1945 Scout box. It was neces-

sary to pinch the two sides of the cap in a bit, on the inside and stick them in order for the cap to be the right shape.

The shirt is made of regulation cotton and closes by means of two buttons on the collar and is called the Gymnastiorka, the 1943 model. Moreover *Dragon* supplies — it can be glimpsed on the left hand side of our man — a *Military Valour Medal* which has to be glued onto the shirt. Our man is wearing new shoulder tabs edged with piping the same colour as the arms which appeared in 1943. They are made of cloth. As our character is a real infantryman, the colour of the edging is raspberry.

The belt is a regulation model with buckle and tongue. Slipped over the belt in front are the 1930 model cartridge pouches, each containing three magazines of five 7.62 cartridges for the Mosin-Nagant rifle. Hanging from the belt at the rear are the spade and the aluminium flask with a cover fastened by two press studs and tightened by a little cord; the former have to be cut and the flap glued with the studs (the self-adhesive piece supplied by the maker does not actually. stick very well). The spade is made of square steel and represents one of the many variations available. Be patient, getting the individual tool into its cover may take time — the cover is cut to exactly the right dimensions of the steel.

The trousers are the 1935 model. This cotton model is recognisable by the knee reinforcement pads cut into a point towards the top. This item was common to all the services and can therefore be useful later on. The regulation beginning-of-conflict boots have been replaced by regulation hobnailed boots and cotton puttees.

The whole is moulded in one piece. This technique has the advantage of looking 'tighter', although the result errs by the lack of realism of the painting — which is a bit too brilliant — and the material. The gas mask bag is carried saltire-wise on the left hand side. Always carried over the shoulder but on the right hand side this time is the khaki tent cloth which can be worn as a waterproof hood with adjusting cords. Moreover an opening in the right side allows the right arm through. You can also place the tent-cloth as a cape protecting the man and all his equipment.

Below, there is a *Myeshok* rucksack, a cloth square whose straps were also used to close it. A little notice tells you how to go about this. This rather rustic design was theoretically replaced in the middle of the conflict with the 1939-model haversack which *Dragon* has not brought out yet. The rifle is a Mosin-Nagant 1891-30 supplied with its short bayonet with a cruciform point. Another bayonet, shorter this time and used as a dagger, has been slipped under the belt.

Our last figurine is a scout from the end of the war, wearing a one piece camouflage suit. Underneath this our man is wearing the same shirt and trousers describe above. His weapon is a PPSH 41 with a straight magazine.

This photograph enables one to admire the precision of the reproduction of the map-holder made of natural leather which was handed out to officers, NCOs, section commanders and scouts. Many different variations of this model were made and different materials were used to make them.

29

THE BRITISH

Flight Sergeant, N°69 Squadron, Biggin Hill, 1941

Our first RAF pilot is very simple. To create this pilot we used the *BBI* box for the Pilot in Western Europe.

To give him that special silhouette, we used a period photograph showing several RAF officers and NCOs playing cricket in the Dispersal Area of the famous English airfield.

From the original box we kept the cap, the service dress trousers and the life jacket -1932 model, painted yellow in the squadron workshops (the grey fastener shows the original colour).

The shoes, the tie and the shirt come from a very modern *Dragon* box containing a Hong Kong bodyguard in civvies. The watch comes from a *Dragon* box as does the figurine.

Flight-Lieutenant, N°33 Squadron, Egypt, 1940

This Hurricane pilot in Egypt who closely resembles Clark Gable is the *BBI* RAF Pilot in North Africa figurine, only slightly re-worked.

The helmet is a D model, the oxygen mask is a D model and the goggles are a very beautiful pair of Mk IIs. The life jacket is a re-worked Type D. all these items come from the normal box as does the battledress jacket and the khaki drill shorts worn by all British soldiers in the tropics.

Be careful, there never was a light

khaki battledress jacket. So our jacket has to be coloured brown as in the photograph. As this colour lightens very quickly, it can be made fairly pale.

Acrylic inks or paints for cloth offer a wide range of ideas. This battledress jacket was thus a model issued to the rest of the army but not the RAF. The loops for the shoulder flaps on which were sewn the rank insignia have been left khaki, which seemed logical to us in the circumstances.

The 1936 model leather flying boots and the big white woollen socks have been taken from another *BBI* box, the RAF Pilot in Europe.

The light leather flying gloves are from the original box. The beautiful, very British neckerchief comes with the *BBI* figurine.

The uniform has been dirtied a little with emphasis particularly on the dusty side of things, using white pastel. Using Games Workshop paints and the aerograph, we have also repainted the pilot's sun tanned legs and chair naine.

The third pilot offers a marvellous mix of civilian and military, tropical and European items. The basis for our work was found in the *BBI* RAF Pilot in Western Europe. We used a photograph of Flight Lieutenant Neville Duke in Tunisia as a model. The brown leather helmet is of the B Type, the goggles are Mk IVs with extra swing-hinged lenses for night flying and a type D oxygen mask.

All microphone and speaker cables and the oxygen mask piping have been kept as with the previous figurine.

The RAF blue battledress jacket is the original one with the signal whistle attached to the collar. The white scarf comes from the *Ben Cole* box from *Dragon*. The large leather gloves are from the *BBI* box.

Ben Cole also supplied the trousers for our pilot. These American officer's Chino trousers make excellent civilian trousers. The Buckskin boots, the famous Clarks were often worn by British officers in North Africa and are made from American boots of the second type issued from 1944 onwards by removing the visible rivets and painting them light ochre. The soles were also ochre.

The seat type parachute, its harness and the extraction system come from the *BBI* North Africa pilot. This splendid set is equipped with a fastener which is a bit delicate to assemble but which is identical to the original.

31

Bren Gun Servers 1 and 2, 5th Battalion, Queen's Own Cameron Highlanders, 152nd Infantry Brigade, 51st (Highland) Infantry Division, Normandy, June 1944

This character was even simpler to create than the previous one. He is part of a pair representing a Bren Gun team. We have here the purveyor.

The Mk II Helmet is from *'Liam, Commonwealth Troops'*, from *Dragon* (ref.: 70173). Under the fine mesh camouflage netting there is an extra first aid bandage pouch. The battledress trousers and the jacket are from the original box. Unit insignia have been added to the sleeves. Instead of the Title, there is a tartan rectangle in the colours of the Cameron Clan of the 5th Battalion Queen's Own Cameron Highlanders, then the insignia of the 51st (Highland) Infantry Division and the scarlet Infantry Arm of Service Strip.

All these insignia were created in the same way as previously.

The colour of the battledress, brown, is typically British and is not exact for a Canadian infantryman, as the box would let us suppose. The Canadian uniform is much greener, in fact closer to that worn by our Major on the previous page. Our Bren Gun purveyor has been given two extra pouches containing five magazines for the Bren Gun. The other pouches issued contained .303 rifle clips. To realise extra pouches, a webbing belt has to be glued or sewn on, passing round the neck, together with a strap of the same material which passes under his arms and through the loops behind the pouches. The buckle must be visible on the infantryman's chest.

The equipment comes from the basic box used for our character. It consists of a belt, two pouches, the individual tool (iron and wooden handle), its canvas sheath, a flask, the bayonet sheath and the bayonet N°4 Mk II, the Haversack and the suspender belts, the anti-gas cape rolled up and placed under the haversack flap, and the red enamel mug.

We earnestly recommend studying your sources thoroughly before assembling all this webbing and straps and belts. Indeed if the fastening system of all these different items seems simple, one must proceed methodically for the final result to be close to reality. *Dragon* has not made any obvious mistakes and neither has *BBI*. Start with the bayonet sheath and then adjust the braces on our man by fixing the pouches, then pass the straps through the belt.

Fix the flask then the individual tool. Adjust everything and then cut off excess lengths of straps and webbing with scissors. In the British Army nothing was left 'hanging'. Having the *BBI* English Commando box at one's disposal, I was able to add a little loop with a clasp for the

English soldier's regulation penknife. This loop can be placed behind the left pouch or between this pouch and the bayonet sheath.

As our Private is the server of a Bren Gun, he carries the so-called Bren gun pouch over his right shoulder as well as his personal equipment. This long bag was fitted with several pockets holding the cleaning equipment for the Bren Gun, a spare barrel and several tools and spare parts for maintenance and repairs. This equipment comes from the box *'Martin, Bren Gunner, 8th Army, Dragon*

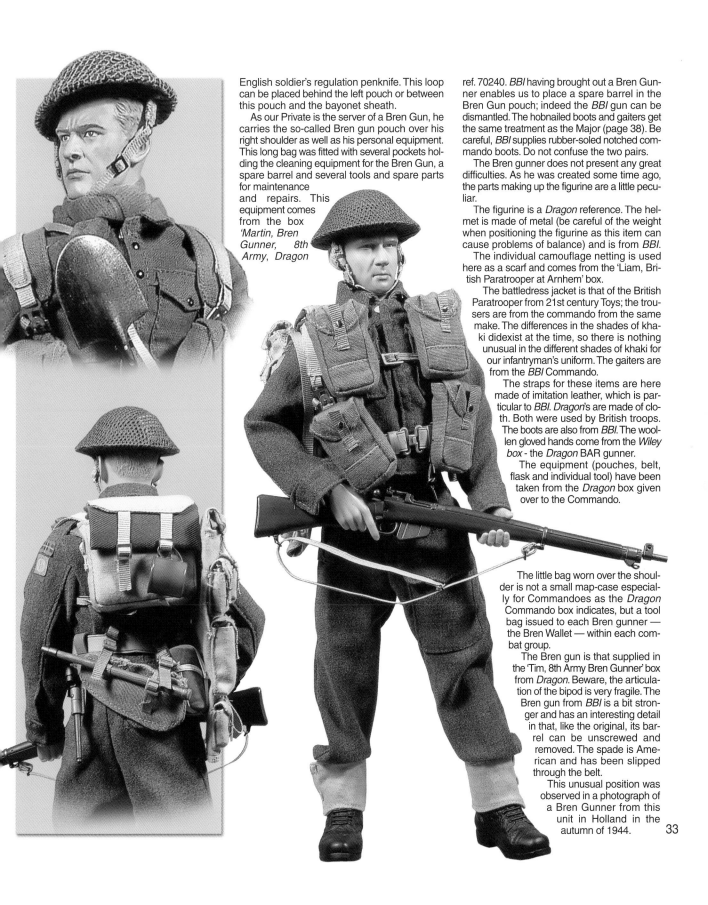

ref. 70240. *BBI* having brought out a Bren Gunner enables us to place a spare barrel in the Bren Gun pouch; indeed the *BBI* gun can be dismantled. The hobnailed boots and gaiters get the same treatment as the Major (page 38). Be careful, *BBI* supplies rubber-soled notched commando boots. Do not confuse the two pairs.

The Bren gunner does not present any great difficulties. As he was created some time ago, the parts making up the figurine are a little peculiar.

The figurine is a *Dragon* reference. The helmet is made of metal (be careful of the weight when positioning the figurine as this item can cause problems of balance) and is from *BBI*.

The individual camouflage netting is used here as a scarf and comes from the 'Liam, British Paratrooper at Arnhem' box.

The battledress jacket is that of the British Paratrooper from 21st century Toys; the trousers are from the commando from the same make. The differences in the shades of khaki didexist at the time, so there is nothing unusual in the different shades of khaki for our infantryman's uniform. The gaiters are from the *BBI* Commando.

The straps for these items are here made of imitation leather, which is particular to *BBI*. *Dragon*'s are made of cloth. Both were used by British troops. The boots are also from *BBI*. The woollen gloved hands come from the *Wiley box* - the *Dragon* BAR gunner.

The equipment (pouches, belt, flask and individual tool) have been taken from the *Dragon* box given over to the Commando.

The little bag worn over the shoulder is not a small map-case especially for Commandoes as the *Dragon* Commando box indicates, but a tool bag issued to each Bren gunner — the Bren Wallet — within each combat group.

The Bren gun is that supplied in the 'Tim, 8th Army Bren Gunner' box from *Dragon*. Beware, the articulation of the bipod is very fragile. The Bren gun from *BBI* is a bit stronger and has an interesting detail in that, like the original, its barrel can be unscrewed and removed. The spade is American and has been slipped through the belt.

This unusual position was observed in a photograph of a Bren Gunner from this unit in Holland in the autumn of 1944.

33

Lieutenant, Parachute Regiment, 6th Airborne Division, Normandy, 6 June 1944.

This figurine is another example of a very simple realisation without a great deal of transformation work. Our aim is first and foremost to give you ideas; there is nothing to prevent you from collecting 'straight from the box' figurines.

We ourselves use several models in order to get the best result and to remain as faithful as possible to the historical original.

Each element which is not used this time will be used eventually later to realise another figurine.

Our paratrooper officer is based upon *'Ian, British Airborne Division, Paratrooper (Corporal) at Arnhem'*, a *Dragon* figurine. But in order to present a paratrooper from the Normandy landings, some changes have to be made. The beret is from *Dragon* and bears the metal insignia of the Parachute Regiment. We have not touched anything here.

The *Dragon* Denison Smock has not been printed with the right colours: they are indeed a bit too light.

Moreover, although the cut of the smock is good, the sleeves of this item, for the period we wish to illustrate, are not correct. During the Normandy landings, the paratroopers wore a 1941-model Denison Smock with tricotine cuffs at the end of the sleeves. The 1944 model no longer has them. Our officer's Denison Smock is therefore *BBI*'s which has the advantage of being re-cut, open and fitted with a zip fastener, which was relatively common among British parachute officers. The Paratrooper insignia on the right sleeve is the original one. The officer's pips sewn onto the shoulder flaps are home-made. For each pip, two half-clover leaves from *Historex* cut-outs were joined toge-

ther. They were painted with gold Prince August acrylic paint. Each pip was then placed onto a paper diamond painted scarlet (the pips always bore the colour of the original service: scarlet is traditionally the colour of the infantry). The whole was glued onto the Denison Smock flaps. Under the smock, our man is wearing a light khaki shirt with a collar recovered from an American officer together with a tie of the same colour. Regulation suspender belts (supplied with our *Dragon* paratrooper) are attached to the paratrooper-type battledress trousers (pocket on the right thigh for the Fairbairn dagger, gusset-type pocket on the left thigh, etc.) from *Dragon*. The gaiters and the boots are the original ones. The leather gloves come from one of the *Dragon 'Hands' blister packs*. The equipment belongs mainly to *'Ian'*: belt, suspender belts, pouches and flask.

The holster, the RAC Tank man, belongs to the *21st century Toys* Paratrooper box. It has been separated from its cloth suspenders; a loop recovered from a strip of cloth has been added to it so that it can be slipped on to the belt. This not very regulation practice has been observed on period photographs (for the right position for this type of holster, see the RTR Officer on page 38).

The Webley revolver and its plastic knot come from the basic box. The Mk V Sten Gun with wooden stock issued to paratroopers is from the same box. The Fairbairn dagger in its sheath which we have not placed in the battledress trouser pocket, but attached to the belt over the Lieutenant's left hip is also from *Dragon*. The helmet (which is not supplied in the *Dragon* box; a *Dragon* blister pack provides it but with a cloth chinstrap) has a leather chinstrap and camouflage netting. (Be careful, the *BBI* helmets are made of metal and can cause the figurine to topple over, depending on how the figurine is positioned). It comes from the *BBI* box as does the regulation flashlight placed in one of the Denison Smock pockets. The strips of cloth on the helmet are from *Dragon* and *BBI*.

34

Private, Devonshire Regiment, 1st Airborne Division, Arnhem

This paratrooper is the perfect example of what can be created with parts from the three principal makers.

The figurine is from *Dragon*, recovered from one of the make's Germans. The helmet is originally from 21 Century Toys and has been covered with netting from an old GI Joe reference.

The individual camouflage netting worn as a scarf comes from the *BBI* paratrooper. The very nice Denison Smock is from *21st century Toys*.

Dragon made one for its Arnhem paratrooper, but unfortunately the colours were not very good and it has to be repainted (we did this for another figurine with acrylic paints and inks and painted for cloth, diluted with water). The Denison smock from *BBI* is the officer's model (see opposite) like that provided for the character from the film *'the Eagle has landed'*. Our character's Denison smock has a real beaver's tail which can be put in both positions. Its only defect is to be a bit short in the sleeves for *BBI* or *Dragon* characters.

The paratrooper insignia worn on the right sleeve is a decal from *21st century Toys*; it is made of cloth and placed on the *BBI* Denison Smock. The *Dragon* one is glued into position.

Naturally as with 85% of all the clothes we use, the press studs have to be removed and the various sleeves and sides of the clothes have to be glued together (cloth glue or cyanoacrylate). Suspender belts, pouches, individual tool and its sheath, all come from the *BBI* paratrooper box. The haversack, cape and mug are from *Dragon*. The *BBI* pouches open, the *Dragon* ones do not. They remain rather soft even when filled. The *BBI* belt here is canvas and metal whereas the *Dragon* one is made of plastic. The first is therefore more realistic but does not close very well; the second looks more like a toy but closes perfectly well.

The special airborne troops' magazine belt, as well as the magazines filling the seven compartments comes from *BBI*, as does the bayonet, its scabbard and the little sheath containing the clip for the Sten gun. The Toggle Rope is the climbing rope recovered from the *BBI* Commando. The paratrooper type battledress trousers (with extra pockets and larger cargo pocket) come from *BBI*. It is the most realistic one out of the three makes.

The leggings and the boots come from *BBI*. The Sten Gun comes from the American *21st century Toys*. Unlike weapons from other makers, *21st century Toys'* guns do not have working parts, but they have a wider choice.

35

Private, N°9 Commando, 2nd Special Service Brigade, Anzio 1944

The first commando which we created was a total rebuild. The basis is the figurine *'Melvin, the PIAT server'* from *Dragon*. The battledress pattern 37 (trousers and jacket), the gaiters and the boots come from the same reference. Do not forget when you assemble the jacket, to attach it like the original with the little elastic flaps to the three buttons on the trousers provided for just this.

The heavy cloth jacket made for carrying the Bren gun magazines comes from the *BBI* box of the *'Commando in Libya'*. The pockets close thanks to little buckles and a bead. It contains four magazines. On the jacket, buckles at the rear enable the individual tool to be attached. On the left hand side there are loops for the bayonet sheath or the Commandoes' Fairbairn dagger.

We have chosen this last option. The items we have mentioned here are from *BBI*.

The flask and its strap is worn here over the shoulder because the jacket prevents it being attached; it comes from the *Dragon* Commando. The Bren gun is the splendid *BBI* model whose barrel revolves and can be removed and replaced. The life-belt is a *BBI* part coming from the same commando box mentioned above.

The woollen Balaclava and gloves are… American from *Wiley the BAR Gunner*, from *Dragon*.

Be careful: all these woollen head-pieces (Balaclavas and other Beanies) have to be dealt with very carefully when you try to remove the excess inside seams which considerably hamper the installation of these items on the heads of the models.

This commando officer here is based on *'Mark, the English Fusilier-Commando'* from *Dragon*. The main change to this figurine was to replace the eternal Royal Marines insignia with something

Lieutenant, N°4 Commando, 1st Special Service Brigade, Normandy 1944

different. Indeed the commandoes were allowed to wear the regimental insignia of their original unit on their green beret. Here our officer originally came from the Highland Light Infantry (City of Glasgow Regiment). The insignia is made from *Historex's* 1/30th parts for plastic models. The whole is glued onto a small piece of tartan which we made

This shot from the rear enables one to appreciate how realistic the *BBI* equipment is, how the regulation machete was carried and the attachments for the mess tin which, remember, opens out. Some accessories from this make.

from adhesive paper printed by means of an ink-jet printer. The pips on the shoulder flaps of the battledress jacket were made in the same way.

All the items of clothing or equipment have been recovered from *Dragon* British Army figurines. The compass holder is from *BBI*; it is supposed to be the magazine holder for the Web Pattern 37 Automatic, but it is far too big for this but it is suitable for carrying the regulation compass. The special suspender belts for men with a hand gun have been recovered from *Dragon*'s *'Reggie, 8th Army Fusilier'*. The Toggle Rope is from *BBI*. The magazine holder as well as the Browning Automatic and its holster come from *Dragon*'s English Paratrooper, as does the scarf worn by our Commando Lieutenant.

The British commando in Burma is an original figurine created from the *BBI* PIAT Server. Our man from the Royal Marines is wearing a very good Jungle green battledress from *BBI*. The only mistake is in the size of the trousers thigh pocket which is too small. Do not hesitate to age the clothes on this type of character, as the climate in the Far-East was not kind to clothes.

The beret worn here is that of the same maker's commando.

Except for the Mk III Sten Gun which is from *21st century Toys*, all the parts are from *BBI*.

Some improvements have been made, especially repainting the identity tags (one green and one red) and ageing and dirtying the items of clothing.

If you want to create these characters from the Far Eastern front, be careful to ensure that your Web Pattern 37 is truly green. Indeed the canvas of all the equipment was wiped with Blanco N°3 which changed the khaki colou-

red webbing into green which was more suitable for the jungle. The infantryman's hobnailed boots have been replaced by rubber-soled boots which were more often worn by the Commandoes, by recovering a pair in the *BBI* Commando box.

37

Major, 3rd Royal Tank Regiment, 29th Armoured Brigade, 11th Armoured division, Normandy, July 1944

Although seemingly so simple, this figurine needed several hours of work.

As the British troops' black beret does not exist, I recovered one from the modern American Army (*Dragon*) Rangers officer. After removing the insignia in the form of the shield of the American unit and filled up the cavity with a small piece of black felt, I made the RTR insignia using *Historex* parts (crowns and laurel leaves) and plastic card (Tank Mk I). The blue scarf is a piece of light cloth recovered from the lining of a woman's Spencer. Our Major uses a pair of American pilot's glasses taken from the *BBI* P-40 box.

The jacket and the trousers from the Battledress Pattern 37 have been recovered from the *BBI* Commando (*2nd British Commando*, ref. 21064). The flap for the Fairbairn Dagger on the right thigh had to be removed and the seam of the trousers had to be taken up a little.

The shoulder flaps (green for the 3rd RTR) have been cut from self-adhesive felt.

The cloth insignia on the two sleeves: the Title of the Royal Tank Regiment, the insignia of the 11th Armoured Division red and yellow Arms of Service Strip of the Royal Armoured Corps and the embroidered badge in the shape of a tank Mk I— worn by all RTR person-

nel — were copied from Jean Bouchery's *'The British Soldier'*, Volume I, printed on self-adhesive paper, repainted with *Prince August* acrylic paint and stuck with cyanoacrylate glue in the right places.

The belt, the armoured troops' holster and the Enfield revolver N°2 Mk I* are parts taken from the *Dragon* box 'Ian, Paratrooper at Arnhem'. Be careful, the holster in its original configuration is only valid for the period 1940-43. It has to be taken apart; the flap has to be shortened to raise it up to the level of the belt in order to get a model in use at the end of the war.

The knot which can be slipped through the belt as here or round the tank officer's neck (regulation-wise) has been made from butcher's string and dipped in tea.

The boots and the leggings come from the same source as the previous equipment. Do not forget to remove all excess cloth flaps with sewing scissors after adjusting the leggings precisely - perhaps the single most delicate and finicky part of the whole assembly.

The captured German binoculars come from a german officer box box, the enamel mug is from the *Dragon* paratrooper and the map comes from a *GI Joe* character, an American bomber pilot in 1944. Under the battledress jacket our officer is wearing a regulation troop shirt without collar from the *Dragon* box, *'Ian'*, and white suspenders made from sewing elastic.

The figurine with nice red hair and a very British complexion is in fact an American infantryman from *Dragon*. A little black pastel powder rubbed over the face (don't forget to put the glasses on) and a light wash made of acrylic chestnut ink from *Citadel* complete this original and unique figurine.

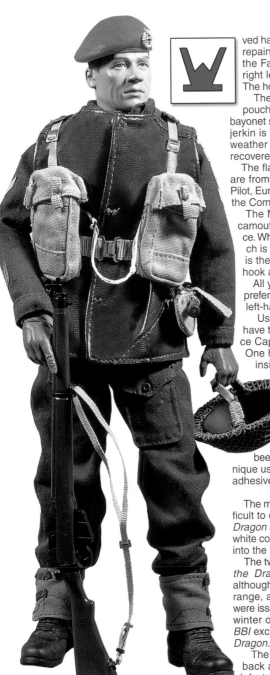

ved hands are from *Dragon* and have been repainted. We have removed the flaps for the Fairbairn dagger and re-stitched the right leg. The leggings are also from *BBI*. The hobnailed boots are also from *Dragon*.

The Web Pattern 37 (belt, suspenders, pouches, sheath and individual tool, flask, bayonet sheath) is also from *BBI*. The leather jerkin is typical of the British soldier in cold weather and comes from *21st century Toys* recovered from the make's Commando.

The flare pistol and the Lee Enfield Mk IV are from *BBI*. The first comes from the RAF Pilot, European Front; the second comes from the Commando box.

The Mk II metal helmet covered with its camouflage netting is from the same source. What is not visible on the photo, but which is offered by *BBI* for its British soldiers is the regulation penknife, its attachment hook and its loop.

All you have to do is slip it over the belt, preferably on the left, near or under the left-hand pouch.

Using a *BBI* Commando beret, we have tried to create a General Service Cap with the insignia of the unit. One has to admit that although the insignia is a success, the shape of the headdress is closer to the khaki beret worn by some motorised units than to the General Service cap. The unit and the rank insignias, and the seniority stripes have been made with the help of our technique using a colour printer and self-adhesive paper.

The man on the right was not difficult to create. The figurine is from *Dragon* as is the helmet. This has a white cover cut from an old napkin, and stuck into the inside of the hat.

The two items of overalls come from *Wiley, the Dragon Bar Gunner*. These clothes, although worn by an American soldier in the range, are of British origin, and thousands were issued to the American Army during the winter of 1944-45. All the webbing is from *BBI* except for the haversack which is from *Dragon*.

The pick has been slipped on the man's back and comes from the *Dragon* 'British Infantryman. The Sten gun is from *21st cen-*

Sergeant, 1st Battalion, East Lancashire Regiment, 53rd (Welsh) Infantry Division, Holland 1944

Our sergeant is a very straightforward figurine to create.

A collarless shirt of the same make is put on a *Dragon* body and then covered with the *BBI* battledress jacket and trousers. The glo-

tury Toys as are the boots. (Be careful: the leggings are moulded with the boots). The campaign souvenir, the P-38, slipped through the Private's belt has been recovered from a German officer from *Dragon*.

THE GERMANS

The influence of the SS (originally the military police responsible for Hitler's protection and the repression of all attempts at rebellion) grew greater from 1934 onwards until in 1939, it became a military force which was to take part modestly in the Western Campaign during May-June 1940. It was only later during the same year that the term Waffen-SS (literally weapons bearing SS) became official.

So *Dragon* has respected this order of events perfectly with this figurine representing an *SS Hauptsturmführer* in the *Germania Division*. This unit was made up of the *'Nordland'*, *Westland'*, *'Germania'* and the 5.SS Artillery Regiments and became the *'Das Reich' Division* in 1941.

Of all the *Dragon* models of the Waffen-SS, this figurine is an exception: he is the only one not to be wearing the camouflaged combat dress which was so characteristic of this corps. In the summer of 1940, there was nothing to differentiate him from the soldiers of the Wehrmacht since he wore the same uniform except for a few details which have been scrupulously copied up by *Dragon*.

The Collar patch bears the small number *2* under the rubes, enabling you to identify the soldier as belonging to the 2.SS Standarte *'Germania'*. Likewise the shoulder flaps bear the letter *G* between the two stars of rank. His brown shirt, a colour which was not used for the Heer's shirts, contrasts with the grey-green of the smock. Finally the armband showing the inscription *'Germania'* magnificently embroidered in gothic letters shows he belonged to this unit. This armband must be fixed with cloth glue; make sure that it is positioned fairly high up on the sleeve (in the first third) as shown by certain period photographs taken during the French Campaign.

These shots also show that the men in the *'Germania'* often wore a helmet decorated with the nationality insignia and the runic shield. As this helmet is rare in the *Dragon* range, you will have to borrow one from *'Otto'* the machine gunner, another *Dragon* reference (70010) which is already old and therefore difficult to track down. The belt bears the SS plate, the other accessories (cylindrical gasmask box, bread bag, mug, flask, etc.) are the ones in use in the Wehrmacht.

Apart from the interest in the uniform, this figurine stands out because of its armament. Although this consists of the very classic MP38 and its magazine belt, the presence of a magnificent Mauser C96 pistol with its holster stock (the large holster even has the screw-driver used to fasten the stock) is enough, by itself, to warrant buying this figurine.

40

Feldgendarme,
Leningrad Front, summer 1941

'Service is Service and an order is an order' is the German equivalent of the old adage used in the French Army: *'discipline is the strength of armies'*. Originally made up of personnel from the uniformed police, the *Feldgendarmerie*'s jobs consisted of duties as varied as traffic control, control of the civilian population in occupied territory, gathering together prisoners of war or guarding captured equipment. It was also resspsonsible for arresting deserters. In the last months of the war when the wind of defeat was blowing over the German Army, the Feldgendarmes continued to impose such rigid discipline that they were given the name of *'Dogs of War'*, not a very flattering nickname which expressed the fear and the little respect that they inspired in the fighter at the front.

This *Feldwebel* (Sergeant) of the Feldgendarmerie was one of the first references produced by *Dragon* on the theme of the German Army. This model has aged badly because of its head which was not very well reproduced (it was one of the first of the series). So it must be replaced by a more recent one. Our choice for this was *'Hunt'* (ref.70214) which has a real expression of authority.

On the other hand, the uniform and the items of equipment show how good the quality of the make was and they end up making a very credible representation of a Feldgendarme. The most specific item is of course the gorget of the *Feldgendarme*, very carefully reproduced here by *Dragon*. It is faithful to the original and it is made up of a 42-link chain holding the silver-coloured plate where the eagle and the buttons have been painted in phosphorescent yellow, as is the inscription *'Feldgendarmerie'*. The 1936-type smock also bears the attributes of the man's job, the specific insignia embroidered with orange thread (an eagle with spread wings on a laurel wreath) on the top of the sleeve, and the armband. The latter is woven with brown cotton and has light grey streaks and gothic letters of the same colour.

The dark green shoulder flaps with two silver stars (*Feldwebel* rank) have orange piping, the distinctive colour of the *Feldgendarmerie*. The forage cap (which we have not used as it is made of plastic) also has piping of the same colour as the distinctive, on the front. The pocket lamp and the truncheon complete the equipment for our character who has as his only individual weapon a P38 Pistol in its holster, on his left hip as the regulations stipulated. This *Dragon* reference has another card up its sleeve in the form of a very useful accessory which straightaway puts the figurine in the right sort of situation: a wooden signpost with a decal stripe is included in the box and you can therefore stick the various very nicely painted and duly aged cardboard signs on to it, unless you want to produce your own and give a more personal touch to your *'Ausweis bitte!'* scene.

41

Infantryman, *17. Luftwaffe Feldivision*, Normandy, 1944

This infantryman from a land-based Luftwaffe division has been assembled directly from the box (except for the head which we have exchanged with *'Leopold'*) without adding any accessories of any kind.

The uniform is characteristic of this type of unit and can be recognised at a glance by the camouflaged Luftwaffe combat jacket, with its brown and green *blotches* on a pale green background. The pattern of the camouflage consists of clearly-defined flashes with numerous dark green streaks on the pale green background. The jacket is closed at the front with five buttons whereas the bottoms of the sleeves are tightened by a buttoned cuff. The eagle on the chest which was in reality embroidered with grey thread, in this case has been printed on the cloth.

The two large side pockets do not open unfortunately so they cannot be filled. Underneath there is the *Fliegerbluse* made of grey cloth; the distinctive green piping of its shoulder flaps and the base of the Collar patches bear the insignia of the simple soldier, represented here by a stylised seagull.

The grey-blue cloth trousers also show that he belongs to the Luftwaffe and adds a touch of extra colour to the ensemble.

This *Dragon* model is also interesting for its helmet, the only one in the range to be camouflaged in green and brown. Note that instead of marching boots, the figurine can also wear boots with gaiters, which are now available in several uniform blister packs from the same make.

Where equipment is concerned, it is the standard equipment of the German infantryman of the period with on his back and attached to his belt, the bread bag (made of blue-grey canvas), the flask, the beaker, the bayonet, the cylindrical gasmask box and the mess tin. On the front, the blackened leather cartridge bags for the Kar98k rifle, all held up by brown leather suspender belts the same colour as the belt fastened with the metal *Luftwaffe* buckle (also be painted blue-grey).

The collector who is an amateur of the Chasseurs-paratroopers could buy the camouflaged combat jacket loose as this was worn sometimes by the *Fallschirmjäger*, as certain archive photographs show.

KapitänLeutnant, U-Boot, North Atlantic, 1941

The elite among the elite, this commander of a U-Boot deserves to take his place on a 1/6th scale conning tower, but for the moment you just have to make do with him in the dress provided by the box. You have to admit that *Dragon* has succeeded rather well with their rendition of this marvellously bearded sea-wolf (another clean-shaven head is provided by *Dragon*). His dress is original at least because he is wearing the three-quarter length heavy mouse grey leather jacket and a white cap with gold insignia of the most remarkable effect.

The other item which is worthy of interest and indissociable from a sailor on the bridge of a boat: the big 7 x 50 navy binoculars which are here faithfully reproduced by the maker. For those of you who have a well supplied leftovers box, it would be easy to give a personal touch to this beautiful figurine by equipping him with red-tinted glasses for night vision provided with the DAK infantryman, *'Egon'*, box from *Dragon*.

Kriegsmarine Stabsbootman, Dieppe 1942

Of all the models given over to the German Armed Forces, this Navy NCO stands out by the elegant sobriety of his navy blue uniform, his weapons and his equipment, adding a little 'exotic' touch to the character.

It was for these reasons that we were happy to assemble this model straight out of the box without adding any other accessories.

Our man is wearing the *Kriegsmarine* cap which is blue and which bears the golden eagle and oak leaves. It is to be regretted that this *Schirmutze* (cap) is made of soft plastic and not coloured felt as is the case with other caps by the same makers.

The uniform is made up of three elements: a big grey-blue pullover with a high neck, the navy blue reefer jacket and trousers. Naturally the most interesting item of clothing is the reefer jacket, with its two rows of five gold buttons (which *Dragon* has not forgotten to emboss with the anchor) and its *Kriegsmarine* eagle which differed from the others by being yellow.

The two shoulder flaps are unfortunately made of plastic but are so beautifully detailed with the crossed anchors and two stars indicating rank; they have yellow piping and are held in place near the collar by a gold button.

The trousers which are three or four millimetres too short would have been better if they had been a bit wider. The equipment consists only of a map case held to the belt with two loops. The belt is made of imitation leather and fastens with a gold buckle. The weapon shows that events have made our sailor into an infantryman since he is carrying a 9-mm MP28 machine gun, a weapon usually issued to second-line units. A stick grenade, slipped under the belt completes his rather light armament bearing witness to the fact that this NCO is taking part in the last sporadic fighting in Dieppe against the Canadians.

43

Gebirgsjäger, 1. Gebirgsjäger Division, Mont Elbrus, 1942

Although this figurine represents the German sharpshooter in the film *'Stalingrad'*, we thought it would be better to place him in the Caucasus, in August 1942 when the men of the 98th Regiment of the 1st Division planted their colours on the summit of the 18 841 ft Mount Elbrus.

But before accomplishing this sporting exploit, our man had to fight with the soldiers of the Red Army, armed with a Kar 98k rifle on which a ZF4 (*Zielferrohr*

4 fach) X 4 telescopic lens has been attached. To be more at ease in his movements, he is not wearing the traditional haversack of the mountain troops. He has just kept the suspender belts which hold up the belt with the cartridge pouches.

The smock with the left sleeve bearing the Edelweiss embroidered on a fir tree green background is worn under the Windjacke.

Dragon has reproduced this item perfectly, cutting it from cotton canvas and fastening it in front with four buttons. To protect them from the icy winds, a buttoned flap on the cuffs insulated the wearer better. The *Windjacke* had four buttoned pockets of which two were for warming the hands in the same manner as the Navy Reefer jacket. The cap is made of the same cloth as the smock and bears an Edelweiss stamped in tin with a painted golden central motif on the left side.

The grey cloth ski trousers (normally held up with braces, available only recently in the *'Soldat'* box) contrasts with the beige-coloured Windjacke and gives the whole the rather picturesque and practical elegance of mountain dress.

The bottoms of the trousers are covered by gaiters made of plastic which touch the mountain boots, recognisable by their characteristic crampons. Amateurs of mountain troops can also obtain another *Gebirgsjäger* in the *Dragon* range, this model (*'Günther'*) wearing the anorak with three big font pockets which has come out in two versions, white and raw silk; the white one is now very rare indeed and much sought after.

SS-Schütze, Kharkov, March 1943

Kharkov... the last victory in the East; the large Ukrainian town was taken back from the Soviets thanks to the cream of the Waffen-SS, the *'Das Reich'*, *'Leibstandarte Adolf Hitler'* and *'Totenkopf'* divisions. For a long time, this victory gave Hitler the illusion that his Praetorian Guards were invincible even if three months later, they were well and truly trounced during the attack on the Kursk Salient.

This *Dragon* figurine is one of the brand's old models and you'll have to hurry up and acquire it for two reasons: first for its rarity value but also for its exceptional uniform. Indeed our SS-Schütze is wearing the fleece-lined smock, the first model with the little hood, reserved exclusively for the Waffen-SS units and which can be seen on a lot of period photographs, the battle of Kharkov being particularly well covered by the reports of the PK, *propaganda oblige*.

The figurine must have its tunic removed however, unless you want to have a fit when trying to get the smock on over it; it is too small and only opens on the top and is very difficult to put in place. The other particularities of this figurine are the winter trousers with knee pad reinforcements, the high top green felt boots and finally the helmet - the only one of the *Dragon* range bearing the runes on one side and the national emblem on the other within a shield.

The figurine's head is very expressive with the mouth open, he seems to be giving an order and pointing with a finger. Instead of presenting him as a MG42 gunner in spite of the attractive drawing by Ron Volstad illustrating the box, we preferred to show him as a simple infantryman armed with a Kar98k rifle. His equipment is therefore standard, the belt fastened by a metal SS buckle, cartridge

Infantryman, VI. Armée (*Feldwebel*), Stalingrad, 1942-43

Even more than the failure in front of Moscow in the winter of 1941, the defeat at Stalingrad symbolised the great turning point of WWII. For the first time, a German Army capitulated in open country after a siege marked by the fierceness of the fighting which reached a level not yet reached in this conflict. *Dragon* has reproduced perfectly a soldier of the VI Armee during the last weeks which preceded the surrender. Wearing the overcoat over the uniform (the jacket has been put in the leftovers box to avoid the clothing being too thick and getting in the way) and felt boots, this infantryman is hardly better protected from the harshness of a Russian winter than he was the previous year in front of Moscow. As camouflage he has made a sort of chasuble for himself cut from a white sheet. With his collar up, he has wound a scarf around his head to protect his ears and neck. The woollen knitted gloves made of soft plastic are from *Dragon* and are too fine for the scale; they have been replaced by *BBI*'s *Gefreiter Dieter Voss's* gloves which are thicker and therefore more realistic.

The head whose face is too cared for, has been discarded and replaced by the head of *Dragon*'s U-Boot Commander whose beard gives the character a shaggy appearance more in keeping with his accoutrement and situation. Armed with an MP 40 whose two magazine holders are worn under the belt, he is holding in his left hand a string of stick grenades. In the absence of strapping, in order to be freer in his movements, his equipment has been reduced to the bare minimum, the bread bag and the water bottle with its mug.

The helmet camouflaged with white paint has been scratched with the point of an *X-Acto* blade. In order to increase the ragged appearance of our infantryman, the overcoat and the sheet have been rubbed with fine emery paper, insisting on the bottom and the sleeves in order to reproduce the wear and tear of the cloth. In certain places carry on rubbing until there is a little hole in the cloth.

The folds are rubbed with dry pastel crayon in shades approaching the basic colour of the overcoat (light green, ochre and khaki) whereas the hollows and the holes are gone over with darker shades (brown and maroon). The cloth is crumpled up and creases created (they can be fixed with hair lacquer); stains are then made with pastel crayons before the whole is given a sheen in the same way as with the overcoat. There is nothing to give away the fact that this semi-tramp is in fact an NCO, with the rank of *Feldwebel*.

pouches, suspender belt and hand grenades slipped in the belt. By introducing little balls of paper in the bottom pockets we have reproduced the padding out of the pockets caused by the odds and ends that any infantryman carried on him when on campign.

A pair of binoculars is worn over the shoulders, inspired by the period archive photographs again which show how omnipresent this accessory was. The woollen gloves come from the *BBI* figurine 'Gefreiter Dieter Voss' and replace very favourably those from the *Dragon* box, which are much too fine for the scale.

FALLSHIRMJÄGER

Fallschirmjäger, Ardennes, 1944

It is easy to change the *Dragon* figurine (ref. 70125) into a paratrooper which will be quite different from the one in the box, thanks to a few simple transformations and additions.

For this you will need to rummage around in the leftovers box and take out a pair of marching boots (any German infantryman's boots will do), a combat knife, a hood (*BBI, Gefreiter Dieter Voss,*) and a coat, that of *'Papa Schulz'* from *Sideshow* (ref. 1903) representing the clumsy oaf of a sergeant from the funny television series Hogan's Heroes.

Before putting the coat on, remove the smock off the *Dragon* figurine and put it in the leftovers box for use on another occasion. If you retain the smock on the figurine, it will become well nigh impossible put the overcoat on the model because of the thickness of the clothing; he has also to wear the camouflaged jump suit jacket.

Moreover, the smock will not be missed as the collar of the hood is big enough to fill up the space between the neck and the collar of the jump suit jacket, whose top button is left open.

The trouser bottoms are pushed inside the standard marching boots, making sure to give them a good ample crease and fold which will cover two thirds of

only with stitching; it is impossible to fill the pockets with all the odds and ends that paratroopers generally filled them with.

In order to rectify this defect and give the appearance of weight in the pockets, all you have to do is insert little pellets of paper inside the jacket on a level with the pockets which will be unseen once the jacket is fastened. The pistol holster, the flask and the bread bag (blue-grey) are positioned on the black plastic belt fastened with a Luftwaffe buckle. The large mesh camouflage netting covers the helmet entirely; all you have to do is tuck the excess netting inside the helmet. Putting the helmet in place on the head takes some doing as the right-hand part of the chinstrap is rather fragile and tends to break fairly easily if forced.

There is no webbing so the Luftwaffe eagle is visible, printed on the chest of the Jump suit jacket.

The paratroopers' thick gloves in the form of gauntlets have been very nicely rendered by *Dragon*, their jointed fingers clutching the FG machine gun very realistically.

This weapon like all the others in the *Dragon* range is detailed with care and is a miniature which collectors seek because it is only available in the *Fallschirmjäger*.

The dagger, attached to the camouflage jacket with a clip on the scabbard, makes our paratrooper look like a commando.

With a few accessories, it is therefore possible to realise a transformation which is both simple and spectacular.

Fallschirmjäger, Crete, 1941 and Normandy, 1944

The other two paratroopers are assembled directly from the box. It is also possible to give them a personal touch by changing their heads or by equipping them with different equipment or weapons.

Fallschirmjäger, Ukraine 1943.

The fourth paratrooper in padded winter dress gives a good illustration of the alternative, only his head being changed for that of 'Sasha', the Soviet infantryman.

To give this the personal touch, his dress is dirtied by painting earth-, sand- and ochre- coloured blotches (*Humbrol* paints mixed and diluted with lighter fuel).

These undiluted mixtures are consequently thicker and are applied to the

the boots; after all our paratrooper must not look like a mere infantryman.

The camouflaged jacket is very realistic, the pattern of splashes have been very well rendered by *Dragon*. The only criticism that can be levelled concerns the pockets which are outlined

boots. All that has to be done is to paint a little shiny varnish in odd places which will give a moist effect, thus imitating mud perfectly.

47

**Afrika Korps,
Obergefreiter,
Gebirgsjäger Regiment 756,
Jebel Manour, Tunisia, 1943**

This model from *BBI* is one of the most recent productions and illustrates very well how much 12-inch figurines have improved over the last two years: superb sculpting of the head and careful painting of the face's details.

Moreover, the items of equipment (belt, cylindrical gasmask box strap, gaiters and puttees) are now made of cloth, whereas those which are made of plastic have been given a realistic sheen, like the figurine's solid Bergschuhe equipped with crampons.

The metal helmet is covered with a camouflage net and the chinstraps are nothing like the first ones from *Dragon*, as can been seen in the inset photograph. The magazine holder made of canvas is well detailed and the MP40 equipped with a leather strap has been given a marvellous sheen.

Behind, on his back, the usual equipment has been attached: bread bag, mug, mess tin and large water flask. The cap without piping bears the Edelweiss of the Mountain Troops and on the front, the nationality emblem topped by the eagle.

All the equipment has been given a sheen by being rubbed down with fine grain paper, the relief of the folds being re-done with pale ochre or beige pastel and then rubbed down, before being fixed with sprays of hair lacquer. The neck is wrapped in a scarf of which one end has been left spread over one shoulder to give the impression that there is a lot of wind.

48

Although we are in the month of August, the climatic conditions in the Libyan Desert are far from idyllic, especially after nightfall, particularly with sandstorms.

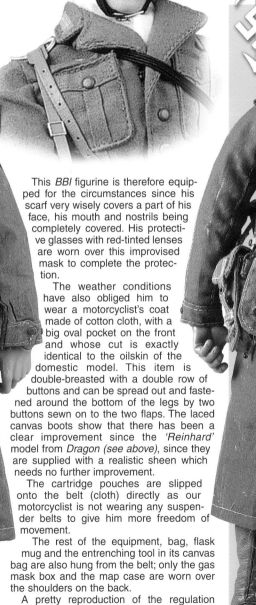

cannot be replaced by *Dragon*'s as that is much too big.

The Kar 98k rifle with breechblock and imitation leather strap has been given a realistic sheen, like all the *BBI* weapons.

This *BBI* figurine is therefore equipped for the circumstances since his scarf very wisely covers a part of his face, his mouth and nostrils being completely covered. His protective glasses with red-tinted lenses are worn over this improvised mask to complete the protection.

The weather conditions have also obliged him to wear a motorcyclist's coat made of cotton cloth, with a big oval pocket on the front and whose cut is exactly identical to the oilskin of the domestic model. This item is double-breasted with a double row of buttons and can be spread out and fastened around the bottom of the legs by two buttons sewn on to the two flaps. The laced canvas boots show that there has been a clear improvement since the *'Reinhard'* model from *Dragon (see above)*, since they are supplied with a realistic sheen which needs no further improvement.

The cartridge pouches are slipped onto the belt (cloth) directly as our motorcyclist is not wearing any suspender belts to give him more freedom of movement.

The rest of the equipment, bag, flask mug and the entrenching tool in its canvas bag are also hung from the belt; only the gas mask box and the map case are worn over the shoulders on the back.

A pretty reproduction of the regulation lamp has been fixed to the last button of the coat. The box also offers the choice of a metal helmet or a tropical helmet on the figurine. Unfortunately the latter is too small and

First Server MG-34, *Herman Göring* Division, Anzio, Italy, 1944

This new figurine is the first representing a soldier from this elite division as he was equipped for the Battle of Anzio.

His camouflaged Luftwaffe combat jacket is worn over the grey overcoat, which itself has been slipped over the smock with collar patches with the white distinctive colour of the HeG indicating his rank (*Gefreiter*).

The dark grey-blue helmet bears the Luftwaffe's eagle and has an imitation leather chinstrap. The cleaning bag for the MG34 like the P38 holster is held on the belt by an aluminium-coloured Luftwaffe plate and the spade has been slipped through the belt as extra protection.

The MG34 is a faithful reproduction with its barrel which can be dismantled, and breechblock. The original head with a rather aggressive expression has been put aside for another day and replaced by *'Kurt'*, the Stalingrad infantryman.

Server Rakettenwerfer Battery, Eastern Front, 1943

This server in a Raketenwerfer unit is sold in a box which also contains the wooden boxing holding these rockets which were the German answer to Stalin's Organs, the famous *Katushkas*. His camouflaged dress, made up of the jacket and the trousers, proves adequately that this type of dress was not reserved exclusively for the Waffen-SS. The whole has been well rendered by *Dragon* who has reproduced the pattern of the camouflage exactly, made of blotches with well-defined edges.

The blotches are green, khaki and brown, and stand out clearly against the beige with dark green streaks background. The jacket has a hood with a white inside, the rest of the item not being reversible. A hidden white slip cord tightens the waist whereas another finer one tightens the hood.

Our server is wearing winter high top grey-green felt boots, the upper and the sole being made of blackened leather. His weapon, a Kar98k rifle, and his equipment are standard but note that the lightened ensemble (allowing him to be freer to move around when setting up the rockets) is not held up by the usual suspender belts.

The wooden boxing for the rockets is made of good imitation wood and the dark green paint of the ammunition has been given a good sheen. *Dragon* has also brought out a box including another server in identical winter dress, but green together with the metal armature which was used to launch the rockets.

So you can create a scene using both figurines, as long as you have enough space on your shelves.

First servers MG42, 26. Panzer Grenadier Regiment, 12. SS-Panzer Division Hitler Jugend, Normandy, 1944

This character was inspired by a colour plate by Ronald Volstad which appeared in the book *'From Glory to Defeat 1943-45'*, a Concord publication. It shows a young grenadier, the first server of an MG42, wearing complete composite camouflage combat dress as was frequent between 1943 and 1945 in the ranks of Waffen-SS units. It consists of a bare model and an MG42 machine gun, *Dragon* reference 70140 'Marcus'. The camouflaged trousers with the *Erbsenmuster pea pattern* come from *'Heinz'* (ref. 70052). However, the camouflaged jacket and the trousers are now available from *Dragon* in two slightly different blister

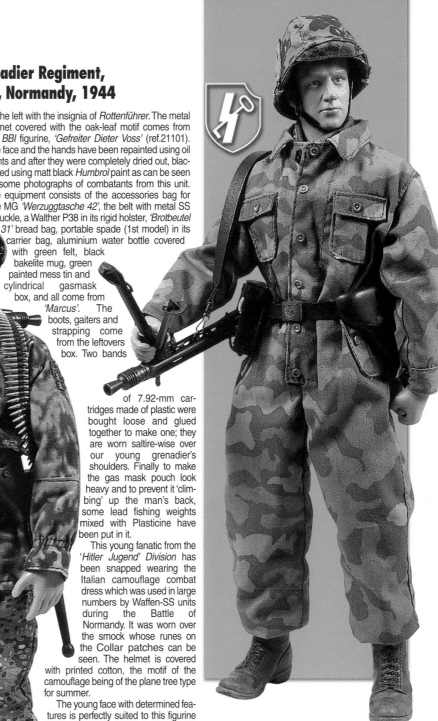

packs, different because of the basic colour of the clothing, brown for ref. 71159 and pinkish for 71158. Giving the characters a personal touch becomes easier and above all less costly. The *Tarnjacke* has 'Rauchtarmuster' blurred edges, predominantly for spring and summer; it comes from the *'Bernhardt'* box ref.70106, and has been repainted (with *Humbrol*) a light brown shade, associated with the green and black, was missing from this smock. But since this reference has come out, a year or more ago, the shades of the new *Tarnjacke* have been improved by the makers and now all paint work has become unnecessary, except for ageing and sheen. The smock comes from the same reference. On the collar, there are cloth Collar patches on either side. They are decorated on the right with the runes and

on the left with the insignia of *Rottenführer*. The metal helmet covered with the oak-leaf motif comes from the *BBI* figurine, *'Gefreiter Dieter Voss'* (ref.21101). The face and the hands have been repainted using oil paints and after they were completely dried out, blackened using matt black *Humbrol* paint as can be seen on some photographs of combatants from this unit. The equipment consists of the accessories bag for the MG *'Werzuggtasche 42'*, the belt with metal SS buckle, a Walther P38 in its rigid holster, *'Brotbeutel 31'* bread bag, portable spade (1st model) in its carrier bag, aluminium water bottle covered with green felt, black bakelite mug, green painted mess tin and cylindrical gasmask box, and all come from *'Marcus'*. The boots, gaiters and strapping come from the leftovers box. Two bands of 7.92-mm cartridges made of plastic were bought loose and glued together to make one; they are worn saltire-wise over our young grenadier's shoulders. Finally to make the gas mask pouch look heavy and to prevent it 'climbing' up the man's back, some lead fishing weights mixed with Plasticine have been put in it.

This young fanatic from the 'Hitler Jugend' Division has been snapped wearing the Italian camouflage combat dress which was used in large numbers by Waffen-SS units during the Battle of Normandy. It was worn over the smock whose runes on the Collar patches can be seen. The helmet is covered with printed cotton, the motif of the camouflage being of the plane tree type for summer.

The young face with determined features is perfectly suited to this figurine so it has not been changed. Only the all-too-clean boots have been exchanged for those of the marine Fusilier of the USMC from *BBI*.

The superb MG42 machine gun is worn over the shoulder and note how the tool bag holds the protective glove made of asbestos used for changing the barrel.

The other item of the first server is the impressive holster for the P38 (the pistol has been reproduced with the same care for detail as with the machine gun); it is worn over the left hip and held to the belt whose plate, painted grey-green, was specific to the Waffen-SS. This figurine from the *Dragon* range is already old and is one of the most sought after, its camouflage combat dress being particularly prized among collectors.

SS-Scharführer, Panzer Rgt. 2, 2. SS-Panzer Division Das Reich, Kursk, July 1943

Gefreiter, 7. Pz Div., Kursk, 1943

The most common mistake is to take any black uniform for that of the SS. This is all the more regrettable since, let us remind you once again, the Waffen-SS only started to exist as a military force from 1939 onwards. The tendency to make this mistake is kept up by the presence of death's head insignia (a tradition in the German Army going back to the armies of Frederick the Great of Prussia) whereas this insignia is only the sad and sinister symbol of the *'Black Order'* within the SS (its design was different from that in use in the Heer). By putting the two figurines of tank crew men side by side, one from the Army and one from the Waffen-SS, one can separate the wheat from the chaff more easily. Before starting off on this little study, let us recall that these two characters are among the most recent *Dragon* references and stand out from the others by the quality of the accessories and especially by their heads which are among the most successful of the whole range.

Although the uniforms of the two characters — short double-breasted jackets and black trousers — are almost identical (apart from slight differences in the cut, the collar of the Heer for instance is generally wider), it is easy to tell one from the other thanks to a simple comparison. If the forage caps are cut in the same manner, the one worn by the Waffen-SS has a silver death's head on the front. That worn by the Heer has braid in the form of an inverted Vee, with pink (the distinctive colour of the Panzers) piping and in its centre the tricolour cockade. If the two figurines were presented bareheaded, all you have to do is look at the Collar patches: if there are runes then he is a Waffen-SS. The death's heads on the collar patches with pink piping on the other tank crewman show on the contrary that he is in the Heer.

The eagle on the shoulder is another detail which is often forgotten or neglected. It is characteristic of the Waffen-SS and is absent in the Heer. Finally the two belt plates are different, each corps having its own model and their motifs are completely different. Note that these two figurines can also wear combat dress, dark grey for the Heer, or camouflaged (oak-leaf motif) for the Waffen-SS. These two items of clothing are provided in the respective boxes, the headphones and microphones being part of the accessories which are common to both boxes. The rather stark appearance of these elegant black uniforms can, if you so wish, be touched up a bit by getting the man to wear camouflaged trousers which can be found in other *Dragon* references.

This sergeant has been put together from the *Dragon* box *'Oskar'* the Panzer Unteroffizier (ref. 70222) except for the head which comes from *'Jack'* the *US Marine RTO, Vietnam* (ref.70032). Likewise we have left out the camouflaged uniform, Mod.43 *'PanzerKombi'* (a little marvel which we are keeping for another figurine) in order to present our character in the black cloth uniform used by tank crews. The face's expression is very interesting and looks rather like an American film

spoilt by this type of accessory, like the heads which were devoid of any expression. The short black double-breasted cloth jacket (*Feldjacke*) and the wide trousers (*Feldhose*) made of matching cloth have been well reproduced. If the jacket has pointed collar patches like the Heer's, the cut is rather that of the Waffen-SS, with a narrower fold on the chest. The collar flaps/boards bear the runes and the insignia of the rank of *Scharführer*. The shoulder flaps are edged with pink, the distinctive colour of the armoured service. The grey eagle on the sleeve is the BeVo type.

Our man has been awarded the Iron Cross, hanging round his neck and worn over a black shirt and tie. He has a single belt with a little blackened leather holster (Walther PPK). This is therefore a rather sparse version of a tank crew member, but it corresponds perfectly with the gear worn in combat where very often this uniform was worn under anthracite grey or camouflaged (plane tree or oak leaf motifs) overalls; whereas in summer, he would be in shirt sleeves.

Finally, the double breasted jacket and trousers were often replaced after 1943 by camouflaged (green pea or oak-leaf motifs for autumn-winter) clothing of the same cut.

This figurine of a second-lieutenant in a Panzer regiment was originally a reference (11.13.91) from the make In the Past Toys showing the very famous Michael Wittman. The model does not actually really look like Wittman. The head is too big compared with the rest of the figurine, not to mention the hands with are also out of proportion. Therefore we have chosen a character, admittedly more anonymous, but with more regular proportions whom we call *SS Unersturmführer 'X'*. For this we have used a bare model, *'Stefan'*, *Dragon* reference 70011. He is wearing a feldgrau service dress Schirmütze; this hat comes from the *Dragon* 71107 set *German Elite Officer Camouflage Smock*. All the rest of the uniform (except for the boots which come from the leftovers box) is that of the In the Past Toys model and consists of the short black woollen cloth double-breasted jacket and matching trousers; the cut and the texture of the clothing are particularly well made.

The jacket has a smaller and rounder collar than the *Dragon* one and has silver piping, reserved for officers, confirmed by the collar patches. The runes and the rank insignia are well done and the shoulder patches made of twists of aluminium, edged with pink, and adorned with LAH in bronze lettering.

The eagle on the sleeve together with a removable embroidered armband complete the model, not forgetting to mention several decorations, one golden German Cross. Our man is wearing a brown shirt with a black tie with the Knight's Iron Cross. The officer's belt is fastened with a particularly effective buckle; he is wearing a very realistic brown imitation leather holster.

star. This head is wearing the black forage cap bearing the eagle and the death's head in grey thread, BeVo type; after a series of inconclusive try ons (helmets too big, or badly cut *Feldmütze*), *Dragon* finally succeeded in reproducing this type of headgear exactly. We hope that the maker will provide us with sets of caps and forage caps of this quality so that we can improve on the old references which were

SS-Untersturmführer, SS-Panzer Rgt. 1, 1. SS-Pz. Division, Leibstandarte Adolf Hitler

SS-Schütze (Sniper), Panzer Grenadier Reg. *Westland*, 5. SS-Pz. Div. *Wiking*, Kursk, 1943

This sniper is made up of the bare model *'Zanis'*, *Dragon* reference 70219, and other elements coming from other sets and the leftovers box. His uniform consists of a Model 43 Feldgrau jacket with pockets without gussets (*Dragon* set 71025) with woollen cloth collar, decorated with runes made of BeVo and on the left, with a simple woollen cloth flap without any decoration. Model 1937 cloth trousers also in Feldgrau and marching boots with grey-green canvas gaiters complete the uniform.

Over the smock, he is wearing the second model of Tarnjacke for spring with the oak leaf motif. This features two large pockets on the hips with flaps, elastic fasteners around the waist and the cuffs. Finally camouflaged loops have been sewn to the shoulders and high up on the back. The jacket is reversible, the other side being for autumn and winter and is almost waterproof. For this jacket we have used the set from *Ultimate Soldier* ref. 34320. The sheen was made using Humbrol paints and pastel. The 1935-40 model helmet is covered with a camouflaged cover with the same pattern as the jacket; straps enable branches and leaves to be attached. The equipment includes a black leather belt with SS-buckle -the troop model made of grey-green steel - two black leather magazine holders for the Kar98k rifle, troop-model suspender belts. On his back he is carrying standard equipment: *Brotbeutel 31* bread bag, portable spade (2nd model) with carrier, flask, mug, mess tin and gas mask pouch. Not visible on the photograph is a dark brown leather sheath containing the x 4 sights for the rifle which has been slipped through the belt. A model 1924 stick grenade is also under the belt.

SS-Schütze, 13. SS-Gebirgs Division, Handschar

The *Cyber Hobby* figurines are distinguishable by their resemblance with historical characters or film stars. You will have recognised *'Schwarzy'* as the first server of this MG34, a Bosnian Muslim of the *Handschar* with a typical fez. No need to go over the weapons of this proud (and muscle-bound) fighter; they correspond to what is to be found in the other boxes of German gunners. Note however the smock whose collar patches bears the division's insignia (a hand holding a scimitar) and on the shoulder the Croatian checkerboard flag reminding you that this unit had Croatian volunteer cadres. This item of clothing is worth wearing without the *Tarnjacke* because it is characteristic and adds to the 'exoticism' of the subject. It is difficult not to fall for the camouflaged jacket: its smudged edges have been created by the hand of a master *"chez Dragon"*.

Finally the other part which justifies the inclusion of this model in any serious collection of German soldiers of WWII, is without doubt the rucksack which was specific to the mountain troops. It has been given volume by filling it with paper tissues. As with the original, it is carried thanks to rather wide suspender belts (more comfortable) and linked at the front to the chest to a cross strap which holds the sack well in place.

If you have not yet made this figurine do not dally as it highly unlikely that these clothes and this equipment will be found in the boxes of loose parts.

This captain is responsible for a reconnaissance unit and is a model made up from a bare model of 'Kater', Dragon ref.70088, bought loose a long time ago (two years ago?). This subject caught my attention because of the expressiveness of the face (which was not the case of most of the other characters of the period); since then the producer has made a lot of progress and we encourage him in this, because whatever the figurine — as with a subject made of resin at another scale — the quality of the engraving and the expression of the face are of primary importance!

On the other hand, it does not have a lot of hair and this is greying which gives him the appearance of an old war-hardened soldier, a veteran of all the fronts. His uniform is made up of a smock (*Dragon* set 71025) with runes on the right of the collar and on the left his rank of *Hauptsturmführer*.

The Collar patches are decorated with an aluminium edge characteristic of the officers. They come from the make *Good Stuff* (USA) which provides all sorts of Collar patches, all ranks, each little blister being accompanied by shoulder flaps (not visible here).

He is wearing a 1st model *Tarnjacke* which he has been wearing for some years now. The autumn side is visible here, with oak leaf motif. The principal features of this type are: very low waist, tightening elastic round the neck (it subsequently disappeared and we have removed it from our

model), at the waist and at the wrists and finally two vertical openings on the chest with flaps; with these specifications it was considered not to be very practical by the soldiers and was replaced by a second and then a third model.

As with all jackets it was reversible with a Spring-Summer side and another for Autumn-Winter.

Our individual has rather strangely attached his Iron Cross First Class on the second button of the smock and it is popping out of the Tarjacke whose laces are undone, an uncommonly stylish thing to do for a soldier at the front, although some photographs do show men wearing their decoration at the front, for obvious propaganda reasons.

He is wearing the *Feldgrau Schirmütze*. This comes from the *Dragon* set 71107, German Elite Officer Camouflage Smock set 1. It is a little offset as the spring ensuring its rigidity has been removed and the plaited aluminium cord does not appear with this model, which was greatly preferred in combat by the officers and the NCOs.

Our man is wearing a white scarf round his neck which is hardly regulation; but it is true that at that time a lot of veterans dispensed with certain regulations.

The Feldgrau Feldhose trousers are the current model and come, as do the calf-length marching boots from set n° 71107 mentioned above. In his left boot he has slipped a model 1924 grenade with a pull out detonator located inside the handle (this comes from the leftover box).

His black leather officer's belt (*Dragon* set 71108) with round silver buckle carries only a magazine holder for the W40 and a rigid holster made of blackened leather for a Walther P38. All this is hung from a trooper's webbing.

Our Hauptsturmführer is armed with a MP40 machine gun and he is giving his orders with every intention of having a go at the Americans during these cold winter days of 1944.

55

SS-Oberscharführer, Pz. Grenadier Regiment 19. 9. *SS-Panzer Division Hohenstaufen* Vienna, Austria, April 1945

This *Uscha* is in command of a section of grenadier-voltigeurs in a Kampfgruppe which has been reduced to a single battalion and which fought tenaciously against the Red Army until its unit surrendered to the Americans, at the beginning of May 1945. This figurine coming as it does from *Dragon* ref. 70251, '*Hakon*' has been assembled directly from the box. Only the 2nd-type *Tranjacke* with blurred edges (*Rauchtarnmuster*) with spring and summer colours and the heavy helmet with its cover camouflaged with the oak-leaf motif have been deliberately omitted. Instead our NCO is wearing a forage cap bought loose and coming from 'Hugo' (*Dragon* ref. 70223). The cut of the headgear is very successful and it is decorated on the front with the death's head and the eagle which have been faithfully reproduced.

The dress, both smock and trousers, is a composite as was often the case at this time, at the end of the war. The simplified 1943 model smock is recognisable by its gusset-less pockets, its collar being the same colour.

The BeVo-type Collar patches bear the runes and the rank insignia. The piping on the shoulder flaps is white (the colour of the infantry), our *Uscha* being a *Panzergrenadier*. His decorations include the Iron Cross First Class, the bronze infantry assault insignia and that of the wounded, silver this time. Attached to the second button is the ribbon for the Iron Cross.

The green-pea motif *Ebsenmuster* camouflaged trousers are part of the two piece suit introduced in March 1944 as the Waffen-SS infantryman's standard dress. The dominant colour is very close to pink: very pale beige and the camouflage appears to be very insipid and is all the more realistic. Boots and gaiters have already got a sheen from the makers so are left as they are.

The equipment includes: a black belt with a steel grey metal buckle specific to the Waffen-SS; a pair of cartridge pouches made of brown canvas for each of the three magazines for the MP40 is held up by black leather suspender belts. On his back the normal equipment is attached to the belt: bread bag, portable spade (first model), aluminium flask and bakelite mug. This is lightened equipment, very typical of town fighting. Individual armament comprises an MP40 machine gun and the famous Panzerfaust 100 carried on the shoulder.

The expression on the face is very well done and the now bigger hands greatly improve the character's realism, which is easy to do with additions bought individually.

**SS-Oberschütze,
Pionier-Battaillon.11**

11. SS-Freiwilligen
Panzer Grenadier Division
Nordland, Berlin, April 1945

This assault sapper (*Sturmpioniere*) 1st Class is wearing standard issue dress model 1943 made of felgrau woollen cloth, trousers and jacket. No part of his uniform is camouflaged which was rare among the Waffen-SS but which was rather common towards the end of the war, particularly in town fighting.

The model is from 'Gross', the *Panzerschreck* server, one of the two models in *Dragon*'s *'Königsberg 1945'* box. His model 1943 Feldgrau smock with its gusset-less pockets (*Dragon* set 71025) has a woollen cloth collar with on the right the BeVo runes and on the left a simple Collar patches; the eagle on the sleeve is made of grey thread; the canvas model 1937 Feldhose trousers are the same colour.

The dress is completed by boots with grey-green canvas gaiters. The 1935 model helmet is bare without runes or nationality markings. The equipment is standard for the infantryman: blackened leather belt with the troops' model SS buckle, two leather magazine holders for the KAR98k rifle, on either side of the belt, leather suspender belts.

On our character's back there are a bread bag, the felt-covered aluminium flask, the bakelite mug and the cylindrical gasmask box. He is carrying a special sapper's pouch made up of a big side pocket containing cakes of explosive and a pair of grenade sacks under his armpits (following a method made popular during the Great War).

These contain a good stock of model 1924 stick grenades.

Wire cutters have been slipped through the belt and complete his assault sapper's gear. His individual weapon is the Mauser K98 and he is holding a magnetic anti-tank mine with which he hopes to destroy a Soviet tank.

57

SS-Schütze, 15. SS-Waffen-Grenadier Division Lettische n.1, Courland, January 1945

The man is a *Dragon* reference, 70011 'Stefans' and has been assembled as such without any modifications. Only a few items have been dirtied and aged using *Humbrol* paints and pastels since it must be remembered, he was rolling around in the snow and the mud. Note how well the face's expression and flesh have been rendered. Our soldier is warmly equipped with a marvellous fur-lined over-jacket; it is made from Italian canvas and is non-reversible. It was cut sufficiently large to be worn over all the equipment, in order to protect the soldier from the extreme temperatures. During the very cold periods, a rabbit fur-lined hood could be worn around the head even over the helmet. Four big pockets with flaps (two on the chest and two on the hips) completed the garment. The parka is fastened with ten grey steel buttons and is exactly like the original. The wide trousers, also padded and with knee reinforcement pads were normally reversible.

Here it is worn on the white side, the other side being camouflaged with oak leaf motifs as in autumn. It is to be regretted that *Dragon* did not make it like 'Zanis's' trousers (ref. 70219). Under the over-jacket, he is wearing a short smock, model 44 (battledress style) with on the collar the normal attributes for a trooper in the SS; *Dragon* has however made a small mistake in putting a death's head on the right-hand Collar patches instead of the runes.

He is wearing calf-length marching boots. He is also wearing a large grey woollen scarf round his neck and he is wearing a very nice light-coloured fur hat with ear flaps, bearing a simple stamped metal death's head on the front.

The rest of his equipment is made up of a black leather belt with dark grey steel SS trooper's buckle, blackened leather cartridge pouches for the Mauser rifle and the leather sheath containing a sighting alidade used with the grenade launchers with which the weapon is equipped.

On his back, there is the usual load of every infantryman, the Brotbeutel 31 bread bag, the portable spade in its beige coloured carrier, felt covered aluminium flask and bakelite mug, mess tin and cylindrical gasmask box (weighed down with a few lead fishing pellets). All this equipment is attached to the belt and is not supported by the suspender belts.

The individual weapon is the Mauser 98K rifle with the *Gewehrsprenggrenate* grenade launcher which could fire anti-personnel and anti-tank grenades.

These three photographs illustrate the various types of camouflaged helmet covers which take up the patterns and the shades of the *Tarnjacke* described in these pages. They are glued and shaped on the helmet by means of *Patex* all surfaces glue. This glue has the advantage of not penetrating the cloth and at the same time taking enough time to dry to allow the cloth to be correctly positioned on the helmet. It is thus possible to create all sorts of folds, looking at period photographs being very useful to get the right effect. We do recommend however to do several test runs on an old helmet in order to get used to this technique, the main thing being to avoid touching the helmet which would lose its paint if it touched the glue, at the risk of staining the cloth during handling.

This *Hauptscharführer* comes from the *Dragon* reference 70106 (*Bernhardt*). Under his *Tarnjacke*, he is wearing a simplified model 43 smock whose collar bears the runes and the rank insignia with NCO edging; this smock is

sand-coloured *Humbrol* paint (H83) wash very much diluted with lighter fuel in order to soften the rather garish original colours and to give the colours less well-defined edges. This Tarnjacke is the second model and is distinguishable by:
— the disappearance of the chest vents and the appearance of two large pockets on the hips
— elastic tightening around the waist, about 5 cm higher than on the previous model.
— elastic at the wrists.
— camouflage loops added on the shoulders and on the top of the back.
A model 1924 grenade with a pull out detonator inside the handle has been slipped into the soldier's left boot. The equipment

SS-Hauptscharführer, Pz. Grenadier Regiment 21, *10. SS-Panzer Division Frundsberg.* Hill 112, Caen region, August 1944.

Div. 'Frundsberg' when this was created in January 1943.
From mere stylishness, he is wearing a rather non-regulation white scarf.

comprises:
a black belt with metal Waffen-SS grey steel buckle (trooper model), and on the right, a single cartridge holder for each of the two MP40 magazines; on the left, the rigid Walther P38 holster. All is held up by the black leather suspender belts. On the back, the standard camping utensils are hanging from the belt, *Brotbeutel 31* bread bag, the first model of portable spade with carrier, brown felt-covered water flask and bakelite mug, the cylindrical gasmask box (weighed down with lead fishing pellets to give the appearance of weight).
Two model 1924 stick grenades have been slipped under the belt. Under his arm our man is carrying the 1942 model helmet, with an oak leaf motif cover. His face is a particular success, showing as it does the features of a veteran of the Eastern front where he fought with the 2.SS Panzer Division *'Das Reich'* before being transferred to the *10.SS Pz.*

from *Paul, Dragon* ref. 70123, bought loose. The other items of the uniform are: 1937 model feldgrau cloth trousers, helmet and high top marching boots, ref. 70106. The pre-dominantly green camouflaged jacket with oak leaf motif comes from an *Ultimate Soldier* blister pack (ref. 34320). It has been given a sheen thanks to a

59

SS-Schütze, 23. Pz. Gren. Reg. Nederland, 2. SS-Freiwilligen, Pz. Gren. Div. Nordland, Germany, 1945

This character was inspired by a colour plate by Ron Volstad which appeared in the album Waffen-SS in action, published by *Squadron Signal* in the seventies. It shows a grenadier armed with the famous *Sturmgewehr StG44* and with a *Panzerfaust* 100, a redoubtable weapon for the time. He is wearing a very nice pad-ded uniform. This composition is realised from a bare model and bits of uniform and equipment from different parts bought loose. The figurine is that of *'Bobby Woll'*, a *Dragon* reference (70019) which is already quite old and whose face has an interesting expression because he is smiling, a nice change from the rather expressionless faces of the period. The body being small, his head has been adapted to a bigger model (*Dragon* has about three different sizes). The padded uniform is made up of a parka and lined trousers with the same features. The camouflage on one side is the oak leaf motif for autumn with shades of grey, brown and maroon with a most beautiful effect; the other side is white. Here are some details: reversible white and camouflaged belt cord, pocket flaps and front fasteners, lined hood which is also reversible, tightening flaps on the cuffs, dark matt grey steel buttons. Everything is exactly the same as the original and is a superb miniature reproduction, just like the trousers. Under this dress he is wearing a model 44 jacket with the collar flaps with the normal attributes of a soldier of the Waffen-SS. The helmet which cannot be seen on the photograph is the 1935-42 model with a camouflaged cover of the same type as the uniform and comes from the leftovers box. The blurred camouflaged cap which appeared towards 1942 is a personal creation as it does not exist in the *Dragon* catalogue. In reality it was reversible, the other face being for spring and summer. The mountain boots with crampons come from the *'Kater'* figurine (*Dragon* ref; 70088). The rest of the equipment comes from the *BBI* box N° 2101 *'Gefreiter Dieter Voss'* and includes a black leather belt with SS grey-green buckle (troop's model), two greenish yellow canvas magazine holders for the StG44, suspender belts also made of tropical-style cloth and two model 1924 stick grenades through the belt; on the character's back there is the usual infantryman's standard load already very well described during these pages. The individual weapon is the *Sturmgewehr* and our SS-Schütze is carrying a *Panzerfaust 100*, the latest model to do a few Russian tanks in, which he did not hesitate to do up to the ruins of Berlin, since the *'Nordland'* provided the very last defenders of the Reich.

Panzergrenadier, SS-Kampfgruppe Hansen, 1. SS-Pz. Div. Leibstandarte Adolf Hitler, Ardennes, 1944

This well-known character did a PK report in which all the people in this group were photographed in a whole series of pictures to the glory of the German soldier when the first victory against the Americans at the beginning of the Battle of the Bulge was announced. This figurine shows an SS

Grenadier, the first server of an MG42, wearing a complete composite camouflage combat dress and clothing off American soldiers. Our figurine is therefore almost a straight out of the box model taken from the magnificent double anniversary set Rudolf from *Dragon* which appeared in 2001. It is very complete and provides two heads of which one is smoking a (captured) cigarette. The Tarnjacke is the 1st model with Eichenlaubmuster oak leaf motif with autumn dominant colours, with shades of grey, brown and orangey maroon. As the colours were a bit too bright, we aged them and gave them a sheen in order to lighten the paint (cream colour Humbrol paint or another shade according to what you want, applied with a clean little rag and lighter fuel or *'Essence F'*).

This was done in not even five minutes; it held perfectly even when given a wash and there was no smell. You have to do several trial runs before getting the right colour. The paint has to be as dry as for a dry-brush. With this method you can lighten or darken the basic shade of the cloth without changing the outlines of the camouflage patterns. If you do insist, you will blur the edges of the camouflage patterns which would be perfectly acceptable with this type of dress with Rauchtarmuster motifs. The principal features of this type of jacket are: a very low waist, elastic around the neck, round the waist and the wrists and two vertical openings with flaps on the chest. The Tarnjacke was completely reversible, the other side having a dominant spring-summer colouring with green dominant. Under the neckline there is a combat dagger, just visible. In keeping with reality, *Dragon* suggests that he wear a raincoat over the Tarnjacke, although I preferred to leave this off as it hid too much of the jacket - you could only see the cuffs.

The smock comes from the same reference. On the collar on each side there are the black cloth collar patches with the SS runes on the right and the rank markings of Rottenführer on the left.

The trousers are a war prize: they are a lightly lined mustard-coloured waterproof canvas model. The steel helmet is a 1942 model with no markings originally. I have put a decal of the SS runes on the right (*Good Stuff* transfers). The face and hands have been repainted with oil. A mouse grey-coloured balaclava is worn under the helmet in order to protect our soldier from the cold in that month of December 1944.

The equipment comprises: the Werzeugtasche accessory pouch for the MG42 with a woven piece of asbestos (for changing the barrel), a black leather belt with silvery grey SS buckle, a Walther P38 and its rigid holster, the *Brotbeutel 31* bread bag, the portable spade (1st model), the aluminium felt covered water flask and the black bakelite mug, individual green mess tin, the cylindrical gas mask box, boots, gaiters and strapping. All this is provided in the box.

In order to give weight to our gas mask box, we have put some lead fishing pellets held fast with Plasticine.

In one hand he is holding a Colt 1911 automatic pistol and in the other a 1924 model stick grenade. The MG 42 machine gun is standing nearby.

Here *Dragon* has created a little marvel of reproduction: the barrel can be changed, the back-sight adjuster lifts up, the breechblock opens, there is a metal cartridge belt, the bipod opens and folds up, the carrier belt is made of brown leather (a rather successful imitation) but the gun does not fire (un)fortunately!

SS-Schütze, 2. SS-PZ. Div. Das Reich, SS-Pz. Gren. Rgt. Der Führer, Russia, 1943

This character represents a simple SS Grenadier. He is made up of the bare model of Alfred, one of the first *Dragon* references which appeared in 2000 and is impossible to find one year later, and clothing and equipment coming from the *Dragon* blister packs described below or from the leftovers box. I was thus able to make a variant of our Alfred.

His uniform consists of a feldgrau model 43 jacket without folds (*Dragon* set 71025) with a collar on the right with SS runes and on the left the simple trooper's rank,

SS-Schütze; canvas Feldhose model 1937 trousers, also feldgrau: and marching boots with grey-green canvas gaiters. Over his smock, he is wearing the 2nd type of Tarnjacke, turned out on the autumn side with plane tree bark motif - the *Platenmuster*. This jacket features: the disappearance of the chest vents, the addition of hip pockets, the elastic waistband is 5 cm higher up compared with the 1st type; elastic wrist bands and finally the addition of camouflage loops and straps to the shoulders and to the top of the back.

This was considered by the soldiers to be more practical and

remained in use until the end of the conflict in spite of the appearance of the camouflaged model 44 jacket with the Erbsenmuster sweet pea motif. As with all the Tarnjacke, it was reversible with the spring-summer dominant colours on one side and autumn-winter ones on the other; it was relatively waterproof.

For this jacket we have used the *Dragon* reference 71111, *German Camouflage Smock Set 6*. The equipment comes from the leftovers box or was bought loose. It comprises

a leather belt with SS buckle (troop model), two leather magazine holders, one on either side of the belt, for the Mauser 98 rifle and leather suspender belts (troop model) with carrying rings.

A 1924-model stick grenade has been slipped through the belt. Behind the character's back, there is the usual standard equipment: *Brotbeutel 31* bread bag, 1st model portable spade with its carrier, the felt covered flask and the black bakelite mug, green individual mess tin and gasmask box (weighed down with lead fishing pellets).

The individual weapon is a Mauser Kar98k. The face and the hands have been touched up with *Humbrol* and with oil to give them more substance. All the equipment and the clothing have been given a sheen with Humbrol paint and *Essence F*, together with pastels.

61

SS-Untersharführer,
Pz Gr. Regiment *Germania, 5. SS-Pz. Div. Wiking*
Budapest Region, Hungary, 1945

This SS sergeant (*Uscha*), section commander of grenadier-voltigeur reconnaissance unit, the *SS Panzer Aufklärungs Abteilung 5* fought the Russian Army until his unit surrendered at the beginning of May 1945. He comes from the *Dragon* reference 70052 *'Heinz'*. Our character has been assembled straight from the box; only the various

articles of equipment and clothing were given a sheen and aged using Humbrol paint diluted with *Essence F* (in order to change the foundation colour of the model 44 camouflage) and pastels. The uniform under the camouflaged item is made up of a simple model 43 smock with a cloth collar and gusset-less pockets.

The closed collar bears the usual standard NCO braid and the BeVo flaps. The distinctive colour of the shoulder flaps is golden yellow, the colour of the armoured reconnaissance units. Round his neck he is wearing a grey-green woollen scarf. The trousers and the jacket with the green pea *Erbsenmuster* camouflage motif are part of the two-piece suit issued from March 1944 as standard *'getartner Drillichanzug'* uniform for the Waffen-SS infantryman.

The dominant foundation colour on this model (one of the first to be brought out by *Dragon*) being represented by a pinkish brown shade which is a bit too dark, it has been softened a lot in order to be more realistic. Boots and gaiters have also been given a sheen.

The equipment comprises a black belt with a grey steel buckle, a pair of cartridge pouches for each of the three magazines for the StG44 assault rifle made of grey-green canvas and held up by leather suspender belts (troop model) and at the back by canvas webbing to prevent it slipping down under the weight. The standard camping utensils are all there and attached to the belt at the back: Brotbeutel 31 bread bag, portable spade (first model) and its carrier, felt-covered water flask and black bakelite mug which have been given a good sheen, a mess tin and a cylindrical gasmask box. His weapon is a *SturmGewehr* model 44 assault

rifle, an exact reproduction, like the rest of this Chinese maker's weapons. The face's expression and flesh is well rendered but despite this the features have been accentuated with oil paint. The model 43 *'Einheitfeldmütze'* fledgrau cloth cap has been retouched on the top in order to make it closer to reality, the making of caps not being the maker's strong point at that period.

These two figurines were inspired directly from photographs appearing in the work '6th June 1944, soldiers in Normandy' using the bare model 'Ansgar', brought out by *Dragon* and 'Gefreiter Dieter Voss', made by *BBI*. These two characters show that as you move on in your collecting, it becomes possible easily to vary the items of clothing and equipment by borrowing parts from standard models or by delving into the indispensable leftovers box. Moreover, certain elements sold in blister packs will be very useful in order to complete your collection. You can then use the infinite possibilities which there are to give your figurine that personal touch, or even create your own character from archive photographs or from reconstruction groups.

This Sturmbannführer has been created from the following pieces:
— Officer's smock, belt and cap, *Dragon* (ref.71007).
— Motorcyclist's oilskin from '*Kurt*' (*Dragon*).
— Italian camouflaged canvas trousers (a set from Ultimate Soldier).
— Map case, boots, MP40 and magazine are from *Dragon* taken from the leftovers box.

In this list two elements comprise the main interest of the character. First of all, the Motorcyclist's oilskin reproduced with a lot of care and available in two boxes, '*Johannes' the Feldgendarme*' and that of '*Kurt*', already mentioned.

This last reference confirms to what extent the SS and Heer officers fancied this article (even if they did not belong to a motorcycle unit); they did not shrink from 'borrowing' from the regimental stores as soon as they could.

Our *Sturmbannführer* (Major) has therefore quickly slipped his on, and wears it open over his smock whose collar reveals the runes and the rank insignia, the belt with the round buckle especially for officers; just these two little pieces in themselves justify the purchase of this little *Dragon* set.

The trousers are made from '*tela mimetizza*', a three-tone camouflaged canvas which the men of the *1.SS Panzerkorps* brought back from Northern Italy in great quantities, in September 1943. These trousers were then tailored in different workshops for the Waffen-SS. As a result several versions saw the light of day and Ultimate Soldier's set only presents one of them.

A little pellet of paper has been slipped into the big pocket sewn onto the leg to give the impression that it is full. The pair of binoculars is camouflaged with jute; they were

bought loose and came originally from the *Cyber Hobby* box '*Jochen Peiper*'.

The other character uses the *BBI* model '*Gefreiter Dieter Voss*', using the weapon — a very beautiful G43 rifle and the rest of the equipment, belt cartridge pouches, gasmask, hand grenades, etc, together with the metal helmet (a *BBI* speciality, taken up on the more recent *Dragon* figurines) and its oak leaf motif cover and the grey shirt, the smock having been put into the leftovers box. So our *SS-Schütze* is therefore only wearing the clothes provided by the *Ultimate Soldier* set: the oak leaf camouflaged Tarnjacke and the famous Italian camouflaged trousers. The pockets have been filled, like that of the officer's, with tissue paper, the open flap giving a glimpse of a magazine. The dust covered boots are supplied like that by *BBI*.

Finally and provided you buy the unavoidable Ultimate Soldier set, you obtain a spectacular figurine which is no longer anything like the one in the *BBI* box.

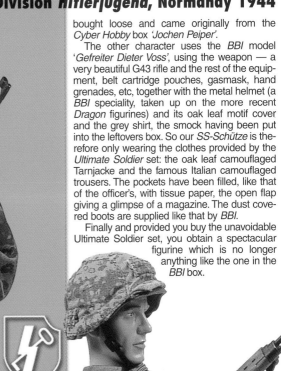

THE AMERICANS

Infantryman, Training Camp, Camp Roberts, California, 1942

Our Private at training camp has been made from a *Dragon* figurine. Our resulting character is the proof that parts from different makes can be used together.

The M-1917 A1 helmet (modified in 1937 by adopting a cloth chinstrap and a new inside liner) comes from the Marine in the 5th Regiment in 1918, from Sideshow. Since the inside liner is invisible, all one has to do is recover the chinstrap from a *Dragon* M1 Helmet, the new model.

The Herringbone Twill canvas jacket and trousers have been taken from one of the two figurines in the Double *Dragon* Box: '*Peck and Hunt, Machine Gun Team, 77th Infantry Division*'. The two items of clothing are aged and worn using white, yellow ochre and light green oil pastels and by rubbing the whole of the uniform with emery paper. The M-1923 cartridge belt and the M-1910 bandage bag were made by Blue Box, the flask and its M-1910 cover are from *Dragon*. The spade and its sheath, both M-1910 models also come from *Dragon*. The spade is attached by a hook to eyelets on the haversack flaps.

The rucksack (M-1928 Haversack) and the straps come from the Sideshow 1918 Marine box. In order to give the M-1910 sack more modern webbing and straps - indeed convert it to an M-1928 sack - we had to add two straps inside the bottom of the sack to attach it to the belt and two little rings on the front straps.

Here the sack has not been completely unfolded. The mess tin pocket on the top of the sack is originally a 1910 Model with a button; for the modified 1928 model, a strap and a buckle had to be added.

The M-1938 gaiters and the boots are from *Dragon*.

The Springfield M-1903 and its leather strap are from Sideshow, the *Dragon* bayonet is an M-1905 in an M-1942 sheath *Dragon*, a little mistake of timing as this sheath was not available for another a few months.

Spades, bayonets, flasks and their covers are provided in all the American models from *Dragon*. Until the models made from 2002 onwards, they were identical and realised in plastic. These parts should be repainted for them to be more realistic.

Infantryman, 305th Infantry Regiment, 77th Infantry Division, Guam, July 1944

Our infantryman in the Pacific Theatre — careful, he is not a Marine — has been made up from the other member of the *Dragon* Double Box: *Peck and Hunt Machine Gun Team, Guam 1944*. The tightening cord for the camouflage net was first removed and then the net was put into place on the M-1 helmet. Once a 'print' has been taken, the net is fixed with cyanoacrylate glue as close to the edges as possible. The next step consists of removing the excess netting until the Liner fits perfectly inside the M1 helmet. The net was cut with sewing scissors and the helmet and the net were both aged. The headgear shown here is that from the latest model made by *Dragon*, and this is an almost perfect replica of the real thing.

We have not used the sleeveless vest from the box but an older one with sleeves and high neck.

Our infantryman is wearing a two-piece Herringbone twill combat uniform, which have been 'worn out' with emery paper and rather dirtied with different oily ochre, green and brown pastels. The boots are worn without gaiters as was often the case in the Pacific. All these parts are from *Dragon*. The rest of the equipment on the other hand comes from different sources: *Blue Box International* for the M3 knife and its scabbard, the flask and its cover; *21st century Toys* for the open magazine carrier (Pocket Ammunition Magazines) and the magazines of the Thompson (the Weapons Special Forces, Second World War blister pack); *Dragon* for the suspender belts (Suspenders, belt, M-1936) the Belt, pistol or revolver, M-1936, the Pouch, First aid pocket, M-1942, the grenades and the Thompson M1A1 Sub-Machine Gun. The Grenades (grenade, Hand, Fragmentation, Mk IIA) with adhesive-tape covered handle were taken from the *Captain Miller* box from *Dragon*.

This view from the rear allows us to appreciate the lay out of our man's magazine holder flaps. Although they are always closed, they are folded back to enable the magazines for the sub-machine gun to be got out rapidly. The realisation of this part by the American firm is interesting, but the fact that it is moulded in one piece is to be regretted.

65

Rifleman, 1st Infantry Division 16th Infantry Regiment, Normandy, 7 June 1944

bat trousers come from the same box. The spade and its sheath, the first aid bandage pouch, the cartridge belt, the flask, repainted by us, the suspen-

der belts and the Bandoleer come from the *Dragon* figurine. The Buckles have been painted matt black and all the equipment has been dirtied with micro-painting and oil pastels.

The uniform has been covered with pastel and rubbed with car bodywork emery paper. Do not forget to treat the shirt (collar and lower sleeves) before putting the rest of the uniform on. Indeed for a more realistic touch, in most cases, with the help of needlework scissors, we removed the pressure studs which fastened the shirt, the jacket and the trousers. Once the clothes were well in place, using cyanoacrylate glue -two little drops are sufficient - we glued the sides of the clothes. This removes some of the not-so-nice-looking thicknesses; however the figurine is condemned to wearing only these clothes.

The boots and the gaiters come from the Zeke box. The grenade, the Garand rifle, the M-3 grenade-launcher sheath/manchon, the bayonet and its sheath come from the *Dragon* box called *Scott* (ref. 7023S).

Starting with *Zeke*, the Fusilier from the Marine Corps at Iwo Jima from *Dragon*, we have made an infantryman on the Western Front. *Dragon* and *BBI* parts have been used. The combat shirt and trousers are from *BBI*, the rest of the uniform and the equipment come from different *Dragon* figurines, with one exception.

The helmet is one of the old standard headpieces from this maker. The jacket has been taken from the Tak figurine of the 442nd Combat Group. As the insignia of this group is neither transformable nor removable, we decided to cover it with the anti-gas armband supplied in the *BBI* box on the 1st Infantry Division Lieutenant. The shirt and the com-

Rifleman, 8th Infantry Regiment, 4th Infantry Division, Normandy

The basic figurine comes from *Dragon*; this is *Bud*, an infantryman from the 4th Division, France 1944. To realise this character, we have used a lot of the latest *Dragon* products. The helmet is still the older model, as shown by the canvas chinstrap with its standard fastener which only very approximately resembles the quick fastening catch adopted in 1937.

The surface is gritty as were the M1 helmets. The light fibre helmet (Liner Helmet M1) is also an old *Dragon* model; the maker's latest model has a leather chinstrap with the clip fastening characteristic of the second model of helmet adopted in 1943 by the American Army.

To change our old *Dragon* production light helmet into a good reproduction, one has to add a single buckle to the chinstrap (first type) or a full 5 mm rectangular buckle (second type).

The paint on the helmet, on the crest and elsewhere on the surface, has been rubbed off (the paintwork on the M1 helmet usually wore off the more exposed parts of the helmet) using oil pastels and black and metal acrylic paints.

Our man is wearing a scarf made from English camouflage netting for 1/35 armour models. The shirt is from *Dragon*, the jacket (Jacket Field OD, second type) comes from *BBI*. The October 1942 trousers (Trousers, Herringbone Twill) are one of *Dragon*'s classics. The canvas gaiters come from *Dragon*'s *'Zeke, US Marine, Iwo Jima'*. The gaiters were the first ones to be made by *Dragon* and were too soft. The second model now made by this firm is now a bit too rigid. We are waiting for more standard gaiters of different heights. The boots are Shoes, service type III issued from 1943 onwards, recognisable by the reinforcement rivets which can be seen at the junction of the uppers and the stiffeners, and by their untreated leather texture. These shoes come from the Hong Kong maker's Tank crewman or the Marine.

The equipment the M-1928 Haversack, here without its upper mess tin pocket, the Belt, Cartridge.30, M-1923, Dismounted, the Canteen M-1942 and its cover M-1941, the M-1940 spade, the bandage pouch M-1942, the M-6 gasmask bag (which can be seen on our man's left hip) and the Bandoleer are all from *Dragon*.

Placing and adjusting the straps and hooks for all this equipment calls for meticulous work, but a lot of time is not necessary. Using tweezers and pliers is recommended. The buckles and hooks have to be painted black or matt anthracite grey. The metal parts of the spade have also been repainted black, brown for the shaft. Everything is then worn and given a sheen by dry brushing.

The Garand M-1 rifle, its bayonet and sheath are all from *Dragon*. The bayonet and its sheath are hooked to the sack by the two corresponding eyelets on the upper part of the haversack flap. Each com-

partment of the bandoleer is fitted with ammunition clips for the Garand Rifle. These clips are supplied with each infantryman from *Dragon* who has been equipped with this rifle since 2001. The cigarette and Zippo petrol lighter are also *Dragon* accessories. They have been taken from the *Sonny* figurine (the USMC flame-thrower server).

All the clothes and equipment have been aged with white, ochre and brown oil pastels. Everything was rubbed with emery paper to give the character's uniform a rather washed-out and worn look.

Sergeant, 13th Infantry Regiment, 8th infantry Division, Brittany, 1944

Once is not a habit in our series and this sergeant has come straight 'out of the box'. Nothing has been changed though some improvements and dirt have been added to make this figurine more credible. *'Sarge, Squad Leader'* from the *Road to Victory series* made for *Cyber Hobby* by *D r a g o n*, represents an infantry sergeant, a combat group leader in Western Europe in

with the Colt M-1911 A1 appears not to be standard issue, but nothing forbade NCOs to equip themselves in this manner. However that may be, the effect is satisfactory and except for the camouflaged hat cover (not really credible in Europe) there is not much to be done to our figurine. A little sheen and a bit of age to the uniform and equipment — this time all canvas — a bit of paint on the buckles and the weapons, a few scratches on the helmet and everything is ready.

It is worth noting that this *Dragon* figurine was directly inspired by a legendary trans-Atlantic television series. This series told the story of an American combat group on the Western front in 1944-5 and attributed to its men a number of feats of arms in fact carried out by a number of different American units of this period.

1943 or 1944. The uniform is correct and the man is wearing the regulation combat uniform of the period: Shirt, Flannel, OD Coat Style, Special; Jacket, Field, OD, second type; Trousers, enlisted men ETO; Leggings, canvas, M-1938, (dismounted) and Shoes, Service, Composition Sole Type II.

The Thompson Sub-Machine Gun A1 together

BAR Gunner, 116th Inf. Reg., 29th Infantry Division, Le Conquet, 1944

Our character is based on the *Dragon* 12-inch figurine: *Wiley, BAR Gunner, 7th Armored division, Ardennes, 1944*, (ref. 70171).

The helmet is one of the maker's older models and is covered with fine mesh camouflage netting. Getting the net with its little cord on, and on the inside (between the helmet and the Liner as recommended by the makers, is almost impossible. The inside Liner does not fit inside completely and the figurine looks totally ridiculous. The cord must therefore be taken off, then the netting set in place on the helmet and fixed with cyanoacrylate glue as near the edges as possible. Then the excess netting has to be removed until the Liner fits perfectly into the inside of the M-1 helmet.

In one or more places, holes can be made in the netting using sewing scissors. The whole is then dry brushed with pastel.

The two-piece Herringbone Twill combat suit comes from the same maker: they have been aged with our pastel technique. The emery paper was used for a longer period than usual in order to wear the canvas down on the knees and the elbows for it to look as natural as possible. The best thing to do is to rub it down until the weft appears. The shirt is also from *Dragon*.

The blue Bandana with a white pattern although not standard issue is often seen on period photographs and has been made from a piece of jacket lining. The patterns have been painted with white acrylic paint.

The BAR cartridge belt, the bandage pouch, the M-1910 spade and sheath come from the same box as our figurine. The canvas items are new from *Dragon* and give a much more realistic effect than the old plastic ones. Be careful, the system for fastening the suspender belts is accurate but fragile. The cartridge pockets have been filled the BAR light-machine gun magazines from the box. The water bottle and its cover, both plastic, come from an older *Dragon* model.

The Knife, trench, M3 and its sheath, Scabbard M8 which replaced the bayonet for the men who did not have the M-1 Rifle, also come from the Wiley box.

The boots and the leggings, made of plastic this time come from *BBI*'s box of 5th Rangers.

The lower part of the figurine has been dirtied with splashes of very fine sand which we found in the railway modeller's shop. The sand has been fixed both on the cloth and the plastic with paste. Naturally, as usual, the equipment's buckles and the weapons have been repainted.

The Browning automatic rifle has been aged by dry brushing the metal parts with *Games Workshop* Metal Bolter.

The strap of the weapon supplied with the figurine has not been touched as we do not yet have anything which resembles leather.

The hands have been improved with a wash of Chestnutt ink from *Games Workshop*.

Machine Gun Team, 30th Infantry Regiment, 3rd ID, Moselle, September 1944

Although we got the idea of doing a team of machine gunners when we learnt that *Dragon*'s double box *'Peck and Hunt'* had come out, this did not mean that we automatically used the same two characters. For the Gunner - or the first server - we chose the Figurine from *BBI*'s Marine which came out two years ago and which very curiously resembles the New-Zealand actor Russel Crowe. For the figurine of the purveyor — or second server — we

used an old 2000 reference: a Delta Force officer in desert garb from *Dragon*.

Naturally most of the equipment and weapons come from the Peck and Hunt Box. For the first server we used the Suspenders, Belts, M-1936; the Belt, Pistol or Revolver, M-1936; the Pouch, First aid pocket, M-1942; the Pocket, Magazine M-1918; the Pistol, Cal.45, Automatic, M-1911 A1 and its special leather Holster, Pistol, Cal.45, M-1916; as well as the Bag, Carrying, Ammunition M1; and the Browning Machine Gun, Cal.30, M-1919 A4 and the ammunition belt.

From the box, for the second server, we took the boots and leggings, the Suspenders, Belts, M-1936; the Belt, pistol or revolver, M-1936; the M-1910 Spade and sheath; the Flashlight TL 122B; the stamped ammunition box, the machine gun tripod and the USM-1 Carbine worn saltire-wise.

The other items of clothing and equipment come from other boxes from two other makers. The Sweater, Highneck comes from the *Dragon Wiley, BAR Gunner* box; the Trousers, Combat, Winter from the tank NCO, 'Mac' from *Dragon*. The First aid pouch and the flask from *Dragon*'s **'Tak'**, BAR Gunner, 442nd/th Fr/Combat Group, Italy, 1944; the USM1 carbine magazine pouch comes from *BBI*'s Lieutenant of the 1st Infantry Division. The leggings of the first server come from the same box whereas the boots —repainted with acrylic paint — come from *Dragon*'s *Captain Miller* of the 5th Rangers.

The combat trousers are from the *BBI* Ranger and the jacket comes from *Dragon*. The two helmets are recent *Dragon* productions as they have a rough surface. The green Tee-shirt is by *Dragon*. As usual, the equipment and clothing have been dirtied and aged using our normal techniques.

There is nothing to prevent the trousers being worn over the gaiters. At any rate, this item of the uniform was very often slipped over the woollen trousers of

the campaign dress. Naturally the armoured troops' overalls were not distributed to the infantry, but the fortunes of war have enabled our man to recover or exchange this very practical cold weather item.

To realise this figure, we were inspired by a photograph of an infantry sergeant during the winter of 1944-45 wearing overalls and a pullover.

The two characters' faces have been slightly reworked using hazel and acrylic black ink.

The advantage of these two uniforms, apart from their being original, is that one does not have to make divisional sleeve insignia, which were not worn regularly on combat jackets and even less sewn onto pullovers.

Directly inspired by the four-angle study of an 82nd Airborne parachutist which appeared in a special issue of *Militaria Magazine*, our pathfinder from the 101st Airborne was realised from the *'Tom, Pathfinder, 82nd Airborne'* box for the uniform and from the *'William, Rifleman, 101st Airborne'* box for the figurine.

Both these boxes are clearly *Dragon*. The T-5 ventral and dorsal parachute and the life-jacket are those available in the *BBI* blister pack given over to this equipment. The rubber assault gasmask and the carrier bag for the Thompson sub-machine gun magazines are both *BBI* accessories. The helmet and its large mesh camouflage netting, the gloved hands, the M-36 bag and the wrist compass on our man's left arm all come from the *Dragon* Operation Varsity parachutist. The dagger and its leather sheath are from 21st century. The white scarf is a piece of cloth recovered from the sewing box.

Rifleman, 82nd Airborne, 505th Parachute Infantry Regiment, Normandy, June 1944

Originally, our paratrooper from the 82nd Airborne was the Navajo radio operator by *Dragon*, inspired by the film «*Windtalkers*». The uniform, the helmet and the jump boots come from *Dragon*'s '*Tom, Rifleman, 101st Airborne*'. The belt, the suspender belts, the First aid pouch are from the most recent of *Dragon* creations. The USM1 carbine with the folding stock comes from *Dragon*'s Nick Korrigan.

The shoulder holster which has sometimes been on American paratroopers is a *Dragon* item as are the dagger, the flask, the M-36 bag and the magazine belt for the carbine. The compass is an accessory from *21st century Toys*. The bandages which were particular to airborne troops and attached to the ankle of our paratrooper come from the *Dragon* Operation Varsity box. All the tightening straps and the chinstraps have been re-cut.

The uniform has been dirtied and worn using our normal methods.

On this profile shot, you can see the very credible quick release box made by *BBI*. The parachute supplied by *BBI* and housed in its carrier case is camouflaged, whereas the chute supplied by *Dragon* for Operation Varsity is white.

The cord passed through our paratrooper's belt has been made from nylon cord and dirtied using not very strong tea.

73

Ranger, 5th Rangers Battalion, Pointe du Hoc, Normandy, 6 June 1944

RANGERS

Here is a Ranger from the 5th battalion a few moments before loading onto the landing craft which is going to land his unit at the foot of the Pointe du Hoc cliffs. Several period photographs inspired us for the realisation of this figurine which shows the complete uniform and equipment of the troops who landed on the beaches at Omaha and Utah at dawn on 6 June 1944. Like on one of the period photographs that we were able to consult, in order to increase his ammunition carrying capacity, our man has exchanged his Belt, Cartridge, Cal.30, M-1923, Dismounted for that of the BAR gunner. The helmet is from *Dragon*. We have operated as usual for the netting (see pages 65, 66). The anti-gas glasses have been made from soft Rhodoid and plasticized cloth. He is wearing a *BBI* jacket, a *Dragon* shirt and canvas trousers.

The leggings and the boots are from the same origin. The leggings are made of plastic used until 2002 by the Chinese maker for this type of item.

The anti-gas armband is made of cloth, coming as it does from the Lieutenant of the 1st Infantry division box by *BBI*. The silk paper technique enables one to obtain the same quality as the original and the same thickness.

The lifebelt and the rubber waterproof bag of the so-called "assault" gas-mask are from *BBI*. The two parts supplied by *Dragon* (*Captain Miller*) may also be used. The magazine belt for the BAR sub-machine gun is from *Wiley* (*Dragon*) as is the metal flask, its cover and the first aid pouch. The items of equipment made of canvas always give a better effect than the parts made of moulded painted plastic. The Haversack is from *Sideshow* to which has been added the mess tin pouch recovered from the Haversack in the '*Peck and Hunt*' box.

The spade, repainted with metal Bolter from *Games Workshop* and green olive drab from *Prince August*, is also from *Dragon*.

The gloved hands come from a *Dragon* blister pack made up of four pairs of hands. The Garand rifle from *Dragon* is covered by its plastic protective sheath made from transparent plastic recovered from food packaging. The little cord enabling our man to carry his weapon is made using butcher's string which can be stained with ink (as here) or with tea. The bandoleer has been filled with ammunition clips for the Garand rifle from *Dragon*.

This time, it was not necessary to age or wear the parts as our man was 'taken' only a few moments before he embarked on the boat taking him to Normandy.

Infantryman, 85th Mountain Infantry Regiment, 10th Mountain Division, Italy, February 1945

Technical Sergeant, 1st Special Service Force, Italy, February 1943

In order to illustrate the Italian Campaign which is all too often forgotten, we have realised two interesting figurines: one straight from the box (right) and one which is totally original (left). The Rifleman from the 10th Mountain Division has been realised from nothing from the model reproducing the actor Nicholas Cage in the film *"Windtalkers"*. The chins-traps have been replaced by others cut from a pile of suspender belts. Under the helmet, our man is wearing a woollen beanie from *Dragon*. The anorak jacket comes from the *Wiley* box as does the standard issue shirt worn under the white clothing. The trousers are from *Dragon* as are the leggings which come from the US Marine Corps box, also by *Dragon*. The mountain boots come from reference N° 70070, from *Dragon* representing a German Fallschirm-jäger. They have been repainted. The gaiters are moulded with the boots and can be removed with a cutter or hidden by the trousers and the cloth gaiters which we have chosen. Be careful not to let the thickness caused by these gaiters appear.

The American gaiters must be tightened as much as possible. As with all American figu-rines wearing leggings, do not forget to increa-se the volume of the figurine's calves in order to respect the general curve of the legs which is high-lighted by the tightening of the leggings. The rest of the equipment and the weapons are from *Dra-gon*. The Garand carbine is a new production from *Dragon* with a strap made of imitation leather.

This Sergeant from the 1st SSF is 'rough-hewn', or almost. We have replaced the Johnson sub-machine gun by a USM1 carbine and added a *BBI* magazine holder made of plastic for the gun's magazines. The originality of this figurine lies in the use of the mountain trousers and the special bag used for carrying the Johnson magazines. A hundred of these weapons had been exchanged between the SSF and the Marine Corps which explains why it was so rare in the Euro-pean theatre of operations. The men in this unit, as with many of the American elite troops liked using the airborne troops' jump boots (Boots Jumper Parachutist).

75

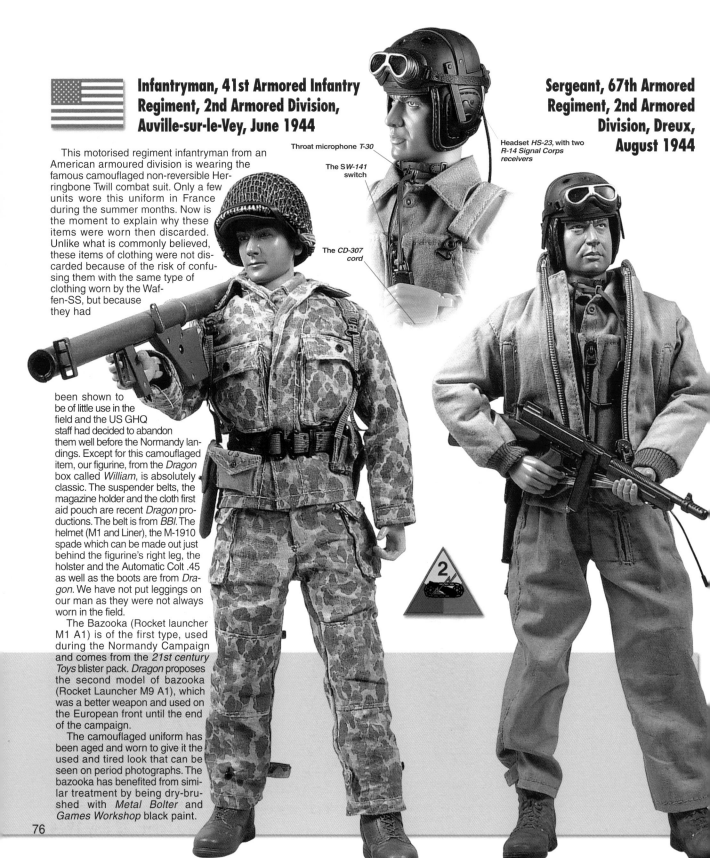

Infantryman, 41st Armored Infantry Regiment, 2nd Armored Division, Auville-sur-le-Vey, June 1944

This motorised regiment infantryman from an American armoured division is wearing the famous camouflaged non-reversible Herringbone Twill combat suit. Only a few units wore this uniform in France during the summer months. Now is the moment to explain why these items were worn then discarded. Unlike what is commonly believed, these items of clothing were not discarded because of the risk of confusing them with the same type of clothing worn by the Waffen-SS, but because they had

been shown to be of little use in the field and the US GHQ staff had decided to abandon them well before the Normandy landings. Except for this camouflaged item, our figurine, from the *Dragon* box called *William*, is absolutely classic. The suspender belts, the magazine holder and the cloth first aid pouch are recent *Dragon* productions. The belt is from *BBI*. The helmet (M1 and Liner), the M-1910 spade which can be made out just behind the figurine's right leg, the holster and the Automatic Colt .45 as well as the boots are from *Dragon*. We have not put leggings on our man as they were not always worn in the field.

The Bazooka (Rocket launcher M1 A1) is of the first type, used during the Normandy Campaign and comes from the *21st century Toys* blister pack. *Dragon* proposes the second model of bazooka (Rocket Launcher M9 A1), which was a better weapon and used on the European front until the end of the campaign.

The camouflaged uniform has been aged and worn to give it the used and tired look that can be seen on period photographs. The bazooka has benefited from similar treatment by being dry-brushed with *Metal Bolter* and *Games Workshop* black paint.

Throat microphone *T-30*

The S*W-141* switch

The *CD-307* cord

Headset *HS-23*, with two *R-14 Signal Corps* receivers

Sergeant, 67th Armored Regiment, 2nd Armored Division, Dreux, August 1944

These three figurines, armoured vehicle crew members, have been made from *Dragon* figurines. The two characters opposite left on Page 54 and opposite, far right, have been made up with the help of *'Mac, Staff Sergeant, 3rd Armored division'*. The one in the middle is from *'Sonny, Flame thrower, USMC, Iwo Jima'*. The sergeant on the left has been made directly from the original box. As usual, in the case of a zip fastener, the buckle is a little oversize. *Dragon* fasteners are a little smaller than the *BBI* ones, but should you decide to change at least the buckle and replace it with a ring which corresponds more to the scale, there is the risk that the fastener, for want of purchase, will not work any more.

The tank man is wearing a Helmet, Tank and Goggles, Resistal, M-1938 with tinted glasses; the lined overalls Trousers, Combat, Winter and the Jacket, Combat, Winter; and boots of the second type with visible rivets. Our man is armed with the Thompson sub-machine gun from his tank's onboard equipment.

The character in the centre, an officer, is mainly equipped and dressed by *Dragon*: helmet, shirt, boots, belt, magazine belt, flask and first aid pouch all come from different boxes of the make.

The shoulder Holster, Pistol, M7 and the gun have been requisitioned from the box containing *Ben Cole*, a pilot with the Flying Tigers; the binoculars come from *Craig, the 9th Infantry Division Lieutenant*.

The figurine's originality comes from the use of the tank man's suit, Suit, Work, One-Piece, Herringbone Twill, OD, supplied by *21st century Toys*. Indeed, several years ago, this American firm brought out a tank commander wearing overalls and jacket.

If the majority of uniforms and accessories are difficult to use, the overalls, the jacket and the jerrycan and the tank man's helmet in the box are very useful. The jacket was for a long time the only one available on the market. This character's boots have been given a light grey white shade with the aerograph, to imitate dust.

The last figurine is equipped very simply with the overalls and a belt and enables us to see some of the equipment details on this maker's very fine figurine. As with the original uniforms, there are differences of shade for the two overalls which we propose. We have 'repainted' the overalls on the left with cloth paint diluted with water. These figurines can be aged and dirtied at will (dust, oil or grease stains). For these stains, we recommend using a more or less diluted wash of acrylic paint or oil paint diluted with turpentine.

Tank Commander and Sherman Driver, 32nd Armored Regiment, 3rd Armored Division, Operation Cobra, 25 July 1944 77

MP, 34th Military Police Coy, 34th Infantry Division, Benevento, Italy, October 1943

This MP Sergeant is not really 'straight from the box'. Naturally we have not changed much, but the little we did makes all the difference.

We have given our friend *Lou* (*Dragon* reference 70279) a woollen khaki tie (*Dragon*), boots (Shoes, Service, Composition Sole) and leggings from *BBI* in stead of the boots with attached leggings (Boot, Service Combat) supplied by *Dragon*. We thus obtain a perfectly credible MP in his role as law keeper.

Two little suggestions for this character: re-cut the black band and stick it to the cloth rather than use the original Velcro. Pierce the buttonhole for the M1941 jacket in order to slip the whistle chain. This chain can also be passed over our character's left shoulder flap.

Be careful! Short of being caught in an ambush, the policemen in these units always wore impeccable uniforms, so do not go and dirty them too much.

Another MP helmet with white stripes and not yellow is available in one of the two blister packs '*US Helmets*' from *Dragon*. The MPs were armed with Thompson sub-machine Guns or USM1 carbines, in which case do not forget the right magazines.

BAR Gunner, 112th Inf. Reg., 28th Infantry Division, Huertgen Forest, November 1944

This BAR gunner from the 28th Infantry Division is in winter combat dress and has been made from scratch from the *BBI* Japanese infantryman who, unfortunately, is not very Asiatic in looks or size.

The helmet and netting, the bits of camouflage and the scarf, Muffler, Wool-knit, are from *Dragon*. The Jacket, Field M-1943 comes from the *Wiley, BAR Gunner box*. This M-1943 dress started to be issued to the American Army from summer 1944 onwards and often rather haphazardly. The olive drab trousers matching the jacket were distributed in the very first months of 1945, which explains why our man is still wearing trousers from the older uniform. Our machine gun server is wearing rubber overshoes, Shoe Pack High, over three pairs of socks in order to get through snow-covered or muddy terrain more easily. These accessories come from *Dragon*'s Wiley box, or all else failing, the *Roscoe* box.

The equipment is a mixture of old *Dragon* products (spade, flask, suspender belts) and new ones (cartridge belts, first aid pouches).

The BAR is also one of the new series of parts from the Chinese manufacturer. Be careful! The makers automatically supply a transport handle for this weapon. Do not make the mistake of placing it on the barrel of the machine gun as it only appears on BAR machine guns after WWII and more especially during the Korean War. The pouches of the belt have been loaded with spare magazines. There again, each pouch is supposed to contain two magazines, but at the scale of 1/6, this is almost impossible unless one does not close the pouches.

everything here is a least probable. Our firebrand is represented by the choice of the *William* figurine who has a very beautiful face of the determined soldier. Moreover his open mouth has a grimace which enabled us to insert a cigarette recovered from the Marine *'Sonny'* from *Dragon*.

The helmet is an old model from *Dragon* and has been repainted with acrylic paint using the aerograph. As at the time this paint did not fix very well we have not hesitated to scratch and peel it. The jacket of the M-1943 (Jacket, Field M-1943) and the white canvas trousers (Suit, Snow, Trousers) of British origin have been taken from the *Dragon* box, *'Wiley', the BAR Gunner*. The equipment and the weapons come from a knowing mixture of *BBI* (M3 *Grease Gun*, Magazine Holder pocket for PA .45 Colt, transport bag (Case, Magazine, 30 rounds with shoulder straps) and *Dragon* (belt, suspender belt, spade, PA .45 Colt and its holster, bandage pocket). The gloved hands are from *Dragon* recovered from an officer of the German Army from the same maker; the boots are here moulded with the gaiters come from one of the *21st Century Toys* of the Infantryman of the 3rd ID in Normandy.

Jacket, trousers and boots have been treated with pastels, emery paper and acrylic paint. A very

From time to time, as with the French FFI resistance fighter, we feel like having fun and creating a figurine which for once is not taken from a period photograph or a description in a manual.

Creating a 'maybe' figurine has a symbolic value and our 2nd Lieutenant in Germany during the winter of 1945 is part of that category. Even if it is close to a Hollywood caricature,

light white veil using the aerograph has been applied to the bottom two-thirds of the figurine. Be careful: the carrier bag for the magazines for the sub-machine gun is provided with two fastenings, but only one, placed in the middle of the flap is needed.

79

Captain, 8th Air Force, England, 1943

(rank, Air Force insignia), the gloved hands and the A-3 parachute bag. The B-5 seat type parachute, its harness, the C-1 Life Jacket and the leather trousers which resemble the B-1 most are from *BBI*. The A6-A winter boots come from a *GI Joe* bomber pilot because those supplied by *Dragon* were impossible to get onto our pilot's feet.

The figurine's most important item is the splendid B-6 pilot's jacket. Theoretically, our man should not be carrying a seat type parachute, but only the harness to which he would attach the spare A2-QUAC parachute in the case where he would have to evacuate the aircraft. But we were unable to resist the temptation to present a fully equipped pilot. The bag is filled with silk paper to give the impression that he is carrying some personal effects, a thermos flask for example as well as his helmet and the regulation oxygen mask. Ageing the leather is without doubt the most delicate thing to do and we have to admit that we do not have any real solutions

If you like leather the pilot figurines and in particular USAAF bomber pilots will delight you. But except for the pilots proposed by the famous make *GI Joe*, you will need imagination and invention to realise a modern figurine. Our captain, a B-17 pilot has been made mainly from *'Skip'*, a *Dragon* figurine.

We have kept the figurine and the cap (whose stiff inside liner has been removed so as to make it more like a veteran's cap), the shirt with the pilot's wings and the collar badges

Doc Peterson is perhaps one of the most beautiful and the most complete figurines brought out by *Dragon*. We realised an almost 'straight from the box' model. Indeed to realise this figurine, we kept all the accessories and a part of our medic's uniform and replaced the Mackinaw jacket by a jacket from the M-1943 dress (Jacket, Field M-1943), the tank man's overalls by combat dress trousers (Trousers Herringbone Twill, Special, OD Shade 7) and the Over-shoes, Arctic, Cloth Top by Boots with attached leggings.

For a more realistic effect, under the combat dress trousers, he is wearing

Medical Orderly, 5th Medical battalion, 5th Infantry Division, Germany, January 1945

mustard colour combat trousers of the first type. Moreover we have filled the pockets with silk paper to give them volume. In a few minutes, that is how to give more realism to a 12 inch figurine.

Dragon's Doc Peterson was inspired by a photograph in *Militaria Magazine* N°71 and has an incredible range of accessories. As well as two pouches for the Medical Service, the special harness and suspender straps for carrying the stretcher, in the box there are two haversacks (the famous M-36 and the one for the gas mask), all the contents of the bags, morphine syringes, bandages, safe-

ty pins, evacuation tags, phials, scissors, tubes of ointment, etc. Naturally the stretcher is stamped correctly and can be folded up completely like the original.

81

Lieutenant, USAAF, Philippines, 1941

Lieutenant, US Marine Corps, Gilbert Islands, 1944

Flying Tiger **Pilot, China, 1942**

The two P-40 pilots, *George Taylor* and *Ben Cole* from *Dragon* (the one from the Philippines and the Flying Tigers) have been taken from the boxes without significant modifications.

We have only added a parachute and its harness, recovered from the George Taylor figurine, to the pilot from the Flying Tigers.

As we said with British pilots, the straps and the belts of all the different items of flying equipment have to be adjusted very precisely. We recommend working closely with period photographs.

The USMC Corsair pilot has been created from the *BBI* model. For the two-piece Herringbone Twill combat dress and the boots we have used those from the same maker's 2001 model. For the life jacket, the helmet, the goggles, these have been recovered from the *BBI* P-40 pilot when it came out for the film *'Pearl Harbour'*. The shoulder holster and the .45 Colt are *Dragon* parts. We have slightly aged the combat dress.

82